MW01592583

God, Sex and Insecurity
(My Incredible Testimony)

Ms. Shameka Bonner

ISBN-13: 978-1456501433

Ms. Shameka Bonner

Contents

Acknowledgements
Dedication
Special Dedications
Prologue

Chapters

Epilogue
About the Author
Final Words

Acknowledgements

I would like to acknowledge my Lord and Savior Jesus Christ, God the Father and His Holy Spirit, for blessing me with this phenomenal gift of writing. I am honored to have this beautiful gift of expression that reflects my heart, mind, and in many ways my life. I offer a heartfelt thank you to Ms. LaTasha Vaughn. I greatly appreciate the time, and effort you spent reading, and editing my book. Your friendship and love is a gift from God. I would also like to acknowledge the prayer warriors and everyone who has helped me in any way to make this project a success. Thank you and God Bless!

Dedication

I dedicate this book to all of my family, closest friends, and mentors who have always seen my potential, believed in my abilities, and encouraged me to walk in my calling.   Without each of you, I could not have achieved this wonderful project. Thank you for your support, words of encouragement, friendship, prayers and love. May God Bless You All!

Special Dedications

To my Mother Bessie with Love; thanks for always being my greatest supporter, confidant, prayer warrior and friend. To My Brothers Clarence and Ken thanks for always supporting me in all of my endeavors. I love you both! To my Niece Shakiedral "KeKe" and her husband Marczalious; two of my biggest fans; thank you for supporting and encouraging me; I love you both! To my beautiful, talented, intelligent Daughter Ms. Hope, thank you for being so patient and supportive of mommy living her dreams; I will always support you and your dreams too sweetie, I love you!

Prologue

To share the story of my life is an honor. However, much of what I am going to share is shameful. Even so, I understand that my life is not my own, and that God has a purpose in all that He has allowed me to endure. When God first laid it upon my heart to share my testimony, I was not in agreement at all. In fact, I began writing the story and quickly moved on to writing something else, in fear of sharing, what you are about to read. God touched my heart a second time to do it, and I felt compelled to do it immediately. Therefore, I know that there is someone, who needs to hear it. I decided that if it would help someone to be healed and delivered, I would not withhold their blessing. Therefore, I share without shame, knowing that someone will be healed, and set free because I dared to share my testimony of God's grace, mercy, and redemption.

Although some of you will read this book with a judgmental eye, there will be those of you, who will tell their stories as a result. The Bible says we overcome by the blood of the lamb and by the word of our testimony.

I pray that my testimony will enlighten, encourage, and help to reveal God's purpose in your lives. I pray that everyone who reads this book will find the peace that I have found beyond the pain, in the arms of Jesus. I no longer cry because of what I have experienced. I now embrace it all with understanding, realizing that everything that has happened to me God allowed it.

God loves those of you whom this book was written for so much, that he allowed me to suffer, so that you too may overcome. I know this sounds strange but it is true. Just as God sent his son Jesus as a sacrifice for us, he uses our lives as a sacrifice for others, that they too may find peace, joy and healing, during their times of storm.

I use to think this entire concept was unfair because I felt that I should not have to suffer to benefit others, but Jesus did it for me. In addition, not only that, but others have also suffered much, so that I could be set free. I will be the first to say, that Joyce Meyer's testimony revolutionized my life.

When I read her books, the "Root of Rejection" and "Beauty for Ashes" and what Joyce suffered, I realized that I was not alone. Both books were instrumental in bringing healing to my life. Her testimony blessed me and now I want to use mine to bless someone else. It is funny that I felt my testimony was not needful, because so many others like Joyce Meyer, and Juanita Bynum had told their stories, and their stories were similar to mine. Therefore, I did not see the need to tell mine.

Then God revealed something to me. For each one of us, there is a remnant of people, whom God has predestined that we should reach. Some of you have been waiting for me to tell my story. Some of you, who are reading my story, have others, who are waiting on you, to tell your story. The purpose of telling our stories is to bring healing to others. We must move forward in sharing if we are going to see others truly set free and delivered.

If God has been so gracious to deliver and heal us, we should do the same by sharing what God has done for us with others so they can come into the knowledge of God's healing and delivering power.

Some of you are not Christians and may never set foot in a church, but my story may be the beginning of something beautiful in your life, that will spark understanding and change. It may cause you to develop a relationship with Christ; at least, I pray it does.

I am going to share some things with you all that may shock you about me, but please know that it is all under the blood of

Jesus now and that God has forgiven and healed me. You do not have any right to judge me. The bible says, judge not fear ye be judged. I pray even for you now, that you will not speak against God's anointed vessel and bring judgment upon yourself. I pray that you will pray for me, that I will continue in the ways Christ, and that He will continue to get glory out of my life.

Also let me add this, there are some disturbing things I am going to share about what happens in many churches. I think this is a good place to express that not all churches are of God. Neither is all pastors called of God. I know some of you are probably in an uproar over this statement, but it is true nonetheless. I know this because Jesus said during the judgment, many will say Lord, Lord Did I not preach or prophesy in your name, and He will say unto them, "Depart from me you worker of iniquity, I never knew you." I will discuss this in further details later on.

Please remember that there are real Christians in the church, but there are also sons of Satan and unbelievers in the church as well. In addition to that, many Christians need deliverance from strongholds. However, instead of turning to God for help, they allow Satan to use them to damage other Christians.

Many of them, along with unbelievers and Sons of Satan (also known as Wolves in

Sheep clothing), prey on silly women in the church and ignorant little girls alike. Please pray for the broken state of the church, and for deliverance, for the men and women of God, especially those in leadership positions.

We will discuss this further later on but now, I am ready to begin the journey through my life, so open your heart and mind, and prepare for the unadulterated truth. I pray that you receive blessings by the power and the anointing of God, as you see Him revealed as a merciful, loving, and just God, through my story. I pray you that your life be transformed and redeemed in Jesus Name!

Chapter 1
The Beginning

I experienced pain and grief before I was even born. I experienced the pain of my mother through the lifeline better known as the umbilical cord that connected us. During the nine months she carried me, I lived my life through her. Whatever she experienced became my experiences also. My mother experienced great pain while carrying me. My father whom she loved dearly abandoned us while she was three months pregnant with me, without any cause.

My mother who had six children and was previously heartbroken by my sibling's father was now facing abandonment once again. Her first husband left her for another woman. My father left without a cause; he simply walked away from us without providing any explanation or indication that he was leaving. My mother would not see my father again until I was around three or four months old.

I would later learn that my father's leaving was due to a generational curse as well. Abandoned as a child, he never fully recovered from its devastating effects. My father went on to live his life-abandoning women repeatedly. I may tell you more about that later but back to the issue at hand.

When my father left, I am certain that it left my mother broken, confused, hurt, angry, and feeling unworthy of love. At lcast I believe it had because if it were I those would have been my sentiments. However, I cannot speak for my mother, but I can say that it certainly caused her grief because it is a natural human process to grieve when there has been a loss. I propose that I too felt the pain of her grief and became one with her suffering as she endured the pain of my father's abandonment.

You may be wondering how this is possible; well let me explain. Think about a mother who affects her child when she uses drugs or alcohol. That child will be affected in some way or another; whether it is by becoming addicted to the substance the mother has used or by being born with some abnormality or defect because of the abuse of a substance.

I believe that just as a mother affects her child by what she ingests in her body; she also affects them by what she experiences during the time she carries the child. Have you ever noticed an angry baby who appears to have an attitude?

I certainly have, and I believe that their feeling of anger, and the attitude they display stems from somewhere, and it cannot be from their own experiences. Think about it, a baby has not lived long enough to experience anything that could cause them the type of anger, which provokes them to toss their bottle across the room, yet we see it happen and why? I suggest it is because usually, pregnant women due to out of control hormones demonstrate different levels of anger among other emotions during their pregnancies that are then passed down to their children.

I am making a point of this because I was always a very emotional child. For as long as I can remember, I was very sensitive and easily hurt. I believe that it all began in my mother's womb as she carried me in pain. I also believe that there was the mark of God upon my life even when I was conceived which made me a target for the enemy.

I believe Satan used my father to abandon me in order to plant a seed of rejection and abandonment in my heart before I was even born, but only after God allowed it. It is ironic that when God allows Satan to do something horrible to us, it always brings life to others.

Think about when God allowed Satan to kill Jesus. Satan thought he had won, when in fact he had lost it all. Satan fears those whom God has chosen; he understands that they are destined to wreak havoc on his kingdom.

Think about how Herod sought the life of Jesus because he was a threat to his kingdom. He was determined to kill him even if it meant killing all the male children who were two years old and younger. Satan in this same way has also sought to destroy my life because I am an enemy to his kingdom.

We must know our enemy in order to defeat him. His aim is to keep us from fulfilling our destinies and callings, but God has a plan to ensure we walk in the fullness of our callings. God does not leave us ignorant of Satan's devices, yet we as believers continue to fall prey to him as if we are unaware that our adversary goes about as a roaring lion seeking whom he may devour. We must submit ourselves to God, and resist the devil in order for him to flee from us.

We cannot continue in our ways knowing that they are sinful and relying on the grace of God to bail us out. Grace is not a ticket to sin but a lifeline for those of us who are in Christ who may fall into temptation. Let us not continue to walk in sin but let us live righteously before our God based on what Christ has done for us on the cross. God is well able to keep us from falling if we trust in Him. I had to learn this the hard way, do not do as I did.

Now that I have said that, I am ready to expose the enemy in my life and to allow God to get the glory for what He has done. He has brought salvation, healing, restoration and redemption to my life and is bringing me to a place of completeness in Him.

Chapter 2
Fondled

Sex dominated my life for many years; which gave me an unbelievable rush that made me feel alive. It gave me a high that far exceeds any drug. It was powerful, empowering, and nonetheless debilitating. I am about to disclose how sex was the driving force behind my disobedience to God and how generational curses are instrumental in many aspects of our lives. My first introduction to sex was when I was very young.

A man touched me inappropriately for the first time when I was three years old. I would go on to suppress that experience for nearly 27 years until about six years ago when God revealed it to me while I was in a counseling session. Prior to this revelation, I had known all along that something had happened to me when I was a little girl, but I could not recall what it was to save my life.

I remember when I was around nine or ten years old, I received a prophecy concerning what had happened to me. I was told that I needed to tell my mother the secret that I was withholding from her so that I could be free. Unfortunately, I could not remember what it was that I should tell her.

Six years ago while in a counseling session, I literally had a vision of what happened to me when I was just three years old. I felt as if I was three again in that same small, dark, apartment that I hated with a passion. I plainly saw the dreadful bedroom where the abuse took place and even remembered how it smelled; like mothballs. The memories began to flood back into my mind as if it had happened the day before.

I saw a chubby man who stood about 5'8 inches tall with a receding hairline and bald spot in the top of his head. I saw his eyes that stared at me with perverseness and desire. I saw his hands coming towards me as he prepared to touch me. I remember how he stood over the bed and touched himself as I watched, while he touched me simultaneously.

I remember feeling sensations but not really knowing what it was. I could not understand what he was doing to me or why. It was strange to me and the only time I would ever experience it was while being at my babysitter's apartment. To this day, I still do not know who the man was or why he chose me other than Satan's plan to destroy me. I believe he was a relative of my babysitter but I am not sure in which capacity.

I never told my mother what I was experiencing because I did not know what to tell her; I did not understand what was happening to me. However, I remember hating having to go there and I would cry uncontrollably whenever my mother would leave me with the babysitter. If my mother had known what was happening to me, she would have never left me there.

My mother was a single mom of seven children and had to make provisions for us. She worked to support us and left my brother and me with the babysitter while my older siblings went to school. The babysitter was an elderly woman in her mid to late fifties. She was nice but extremely boring. She had a small one-bedroom project apartment in the same complex as my family and I.

Things were tough back then and my mother got the best care for us that she could afford. I thank God for not allowing the man to rape me. The most he ever did was touch my private parts and play with him-self in front of me. Nonetheless, it was an awful thing for me to experience and witness; it would later have a devastating effect on me in addition to what was coming next.

When I was five years old, I had a cousin who began to fondle me whenever he would spend the night at our house, which was often. He loved coming to our house and I believe his purpose for coming was to get his thrills touching me. He would touch my private parts, climb up on my back, and gyrate on top of me late at night while everyone else was asleep.

While in daycare during that same period, I had a little girl who would climb on top of me during naptime and gyrate just as my cousin would. Like clockwork, as soon as the lights went down she would climb on top of me and have her way. We were too young to know anything about sex so I figure that little girl had experienced molestation herself. I was relieved when they caught her and never allowed her to sleep next to me again. Trust me, I did not like her being on top of me and would have loved to make her stop but I was afraid of that chubby little girl. She was a bully in our daycare.

I know these occurrences seem so small and insignificant but they were not. These occurrences developed an awareness of sex in my young life. By the time I was eight years old, I was already having sexual desires. I did not desire to have sex literally but I desired to be touched because I had become accustomed to it. I liked the way it made me feel. Isn't that just like sin, it feels so good that it causes you to want more of it. Sin is addictive like a drug and provides a high that blinds us to the truth of what it is doing to us.

As in the case of a drug addict, they become so dependent on the drug, that they need it in order to function in their everyday lives. The drug becomes so dominant in their lives that their sole purpose in life is to obtain more of the drug at all costs.

Sin is the same way, when Christians are caught up in sin, it feels so good but we soon find ourselves dependent and going through withdrawals when we cannot have it as we fight to overcome our flesh.

So there I was, eight years old, totally attracted to boys and desiring to be touched. My desires would soon be fulfilled and in the most unlikely place, the church. It all began when we started going to a new church, which I loved so much because it had many young people. The church I attended prior to that was full of men, women, and hardly any children.

It was not long before I began to take notice of boys and them of me. It was also at this particular church where I learned that men were also taking notice of me. I now know it was a scent released upon me by the enemy. It is similar to the mark of God but it serves a different purpose. I believe Satan smears a scent on certain individuals to attract a certain kind of person to them. I will explain this further later.

So let us go deeper now. I will provide information but I will not provide names of individuals who were involved in these acts to protect their identities. I feel it is up to them to tell their own stories and expose themselves if they feel compelled to do so. My focus is not on those who hurt me or what they did to me. Instead, it is on what the enemy was trying to accomplish in my life.

I will not tell everything that happened but I will give some highlights and examples of the things I experienced during that time; especially the things that ultimately led up to my being raped which was the beginning of many things to come.

Boys and men in the church fondled me often. I recall once when we went on a trip with the church, which we did quite often. We would travel to different cities for conferences and Holy Convocations etc. I always enjoyed those trips because it was a time of bonding and "touching."

I remember the first time it happened. I was sitting on the bus next to an older young man from the church. I remember that after we had travelled a while, he took out a blanket and placed it over both of us. It is sad that I was even allowed to sit with this young man but unfortunately, at times adults are too preoccupied to pay attention to what is happening right underneath their noses.

The young man pretended to be asleep while he caressed my legs and thighs underneath the blanket. It was not long before his hand was underneath my dress and inside of my underwear. He began to rub me gently and it was unlike anything I had ever experienced before in my life.

I had been touched before, but never with my clothes off. Well let me take that back, my bare skin had been touched when I was three but it was different from this experience. My molester at that time never placed his finger inside of my private. So no one had ever touched my inside parts like this and it felt amazing. I was so in love with the feeling, it excited me. I had no idea what was really happening to me but what I did know, was that it felt good and I liked it; a lot. He did this several times while we were traveling on this trip and I loved every moment of it. I recall hardly being able to stand waiting for him to place the blanket over us again so that he could touch me and give that wonderful sensation that made me feel so good.

It was not long after that, that it happened to me again with another older young man from the church in almost the exact same manner. I was ignorant to the fact that I should not be allowing them to touch me. I never opposed anyone who decided to touch me because I liked it and I did not understand that it was wrong.

I should have known it was not right because why would they have to hide it if it were okay. I was so ignorant that I did not understand the fact that someone had already been touching me should have disqualified anyone else the same privileges of exploring my body. I was naive, especially about things of this nature because my mother never discussed sex or anything pertaining to sex with us. I was clueless.

I did not know it was wrong for anyone to get on top of me and gyrate. Nor did I know that it was inappropriate for anyone to place their hand underneath my clothes and fondle me. I just did not know any better at the time. However, by the time I found out it was not right, I was already too involved to turn back.

Therefore, my first little boyfriend was the first boy I ever kissed or held close. He had an older brother who must have been teaching him what to do because he knew exactly what to do when we would come together; I would just follow his lead.

He would hold me close while rubbing on my behind and kissing me simultaneously. We would kiss wildly and even passionately at nine years old as if we knew what we were doing. We would create private moments for ourselves just so we could hold one another and kiss. When I think back on it now, it was crazy what I was doing but I just did not know any better.

It was not long before I developed a crush on an older guy that would lead to a fateful Sunday morning encounter that would change my life forever. However, before I talk about the rape, I would like to discuss the state of the church. I would also like to talk about what was happening to me spiritually during that time.

Chapter 2 Commentary

When I think about being as young as I was having a desire to be touched and allowing myself to be touched, I realize that there was a serious problem early on in my life. I knew that there had to be a reason for this incredible desire for something I really knew nothing about.

I now know it was a generational curse. Generational curses are judgments passed on to individuals because of sins perpetuated in a family in a number of generations. When the enemy has been given access to a bloodline through someone in that line that has involved himself or herself in some type of agreement or pact with Satan, it is manifested even through future generations.

The enemy believes he has a right to that individual because of their grandmother or great, great grandmother who was involved in some type of ritualistic practices that were occulted or demonic in nature.

In my case, I believe someone down the line had to be involved in ritualistic sex practices or something of that nature for the sexual curses that have manifested within my family to be happening.

Rape and molestation has been lingering around the women of this family for decades. Too many of us have experienced one or the other or both. Why would this cycle continue from one generation to the next if it were not a curse of the generations? The bible says, in Exodus 20, "I, the LORD your God, am a jealous God, punishing the children for the sin of the fathers to the third and fourth generation of those who hate me, but showing love to a thousand generations of those who love me and keep my commandments."

What had my ancestors done? Why did I have to face this sexual sin and fight to overcome it? God knows I have always loved him but I have always struggled with my love for sex and intimacy. I have fought constantly to overcome it but it was as if it was demonic almost. It has been like a shadow or a fog that overtakes me and tries to inhabit me. I feel like I become one with sex. Sex seems real to me like a person. I could smell it, taste it, touch it, and hear it calling for me; it played in my mind like a movie.

I never had to watch porn to get excited or to feel the longings for sex. It was a built in movie in my mind always starring some known or unknown man and myself. Most days of my life involved sex. Sex was present in my life one way or another, either by being involved in the act itself, having the thought of it or the longing for it.

I believe that my desires for sexual gratification on every level was abnormal especially having desires for it so early on. I am convinced that I was a victim of a generational curse passed down to me from a sinful act that began generations ago.

I would like to address what happened to me in the church. What I experienced in the house of God at the hands of humans was not right. However, I do not lay charge to God for what man did. Many times the actions of others turn people away from the church and God but not me. I realize that not everyone in the church is a Christian and no one is perfect even if one has a relationship with God. Yet so many people are quick to judge the actions of another without first considering themselves. I am not in any way trying to excuse their behavior but trying to get you to see that it is not for you or me to judge them but God.

Now I would like to address the men in the church who touch young girls inappropriately and have sex with them or other men's wives. Satan is cunning and subtle; he perverts everything beautiful that God has created. Sex and intimacy is a beautiful thing but Satan uses it to bring dishonor on men and women and as a tool to cause people to be outside of the will of God.

Satan often uses men in the church that need deliverance from sex demons, perverse spirits, and past inappropriate sexual encounters to operate under the control of evil spirits and act inappropriately themselves. Many of them are victims who never exposed it to anyone and they have lived with the hurt and scars of the injustice done to them. They usually go on to inflict the same hurtful scars upon others; a negative perverse cycle birthed by Satan.

Men many times are incapable of expressing feelings especially those of hurt and injustices inflicted upon them. They struggle with the idea of admitting that someone hurt them. Instead of admitting that they need help they hide behind a façade of strength and position. Because of their brokenness, they seek only to gain status and position in every way possible.

One way they achieve this is through their pursuit of women and being able to conquer them. They take advantage of weak or unsuspecting women by preying on their insecurities, ignorance, and low self-esteem. They use their weakness to gain strength for their own weakness. The weak prey on the weak to gain strength and a feeling of power.

They have felt powerless but now they are taking back their power by taking others innocence. We need to pray for the men in the church. Pray for women as well who have been victims of these instances and even those who are predators themselves. I will talk about the state of the church in the next chapter before moving on with my story.

Prayer:

Father God in the name of Jesus, I pray for every person who has been a victim of sexual perversion. I pray for their deliverance and healing from the scars that were left upon their hearts after years of pain and carrying the secret. I pray for those who are hiding behind their pain. I pray that you will give them strength, wisdom, and the ability to forgive themselves and others who has hurt them. I pray that those whom they have hurt will be able to forgive them. Lord touch the men and women who belong to you, but who have not been delivered from these ungodly behaviors and practices. I pray that they will seek you for their healing and trust you for their wholeness in Jesus name I pray, Amen.

Chapter 3
A Broken State

My heart is broken because of the state of the church. Today we see so many outrageous things happening in the church to the point of being ridiculous; things that normally set the church apart from the world such as sanctification is no longer a factor in many churches. It is difficult to watch but many churches have become too commercial, appealing to the masses with their fancy gadgets and worldly programming. Most of what occurs today in the church has nothing to do with Christ. Much of what happens is not for the sake of Jesus and ministry but for the sake of members and money.

How did we get here? How did pastors become natural and spiritual pimps, whores, and prostitutes? Many of them are nothing more than spiritual adulterers who are sleeping with the enemy. Those pastors who have decided to lie with Satan in order to gain worldly possessions, members, and status has contracted the disease called Spiritual Aids. I refer to what is happening in the church as the AIDS Epidemic in the Church. It is deadly, devastating to the entire body of Christ and highly contagious. I will talk about this epidemic in details in another book that I am currently writing to expose this horrible epidemic.

However, I will say this concerning it; it is the reason why so many Christians are weak; this disease causes them to be susceptible to sin and its effects and has damaged their spiritual immune systems. However, God is a healer of all things both naturally and spiritually. Therefore, there is hope for all.

With that said, it is possible for someone to minister the gospel, and still live in sin, therefore disobedient to God. It is sad to say, but because of compromising pastors and churches, many are deceived. People are living against the will of God because they follow their leader's bad example. Many churches are now allowing secular and unholy things to happen in their churches and God is displeased.

What fellowship does light have with darkness? When did it become ok for things of the world such as secular music to integrate into the church? My heart grieves for the state of the church. These days, everyone is a Christian by name but very few by deeds. What I mean by this, is that so many are caught up in their flesh and living life according to what feels good to the flesh that they are not concerned about who they are affecting along the way. Their lifestyle is causing others to fall and turn away from God. Their lack of self-control and discernment of spiritual things is hurting those to whom they minister.

Please do not be alarmed because God is well aware of all things that happen upon the earth. There is nothing new under the sun and God has always had a way of dealing with issues such as these when they have occurred in history. I pray that God has mercy on America. I pray that she does not meet the same fate as a Sodom and Gomorrah.

God is all knowing. God knew these things would be so and He has a remnant of people who will make a stand for righteousness and truth. I pray that you are one of them. I pray that you be strengthened to walk out your life and relationship with God according to His will, purpose and plan. Do not be discouraged by what others are doing or not doing because we all have to answer to God for ourselves.

I see everything from cursing, lying, cheating, backbiting, fornicating, adultery, stealing and the like in the church as if we are dealing with ungodly people. I see churches playing secular music, dancing, shacking (people living together who are not married), and homosexuality.

Pastors are sleeping with their members and stealing money from the church. The church has become a big business. The saddest thing of all is that it is difficult to determine whom to trust as leaders any more. So many underhanded schemes are happening until you are unsure whom to believe. I encourage you to do as the Bible says, "Do not put your trust in man, but trust in God." Also do as the Apostle Paul says, follow those leaders who are following Christ. If you do not see a pattern of Christ, do not follow them.

Even demons know the word of God but it does not qualify them to shepherd your soul. Also, be mindful that Satan disguises himself as an angel of light. Satan is not going to say to you, "Hey it is me Satan, and I have come to destroy you." He is going to try to deceive you with flattery, possessions and status. Be careful not to be caught up in the ignorance of many. The people of God die spiritually because of a lack of knowledge.

The church is in an awful state but God is going to deliver His church. He is coming back for a church (Bride) without a spot or wrinkle. He is going to deliver His body, his bride. I reiterate please pray for the broken state of the church that God will deliver, heal, and set free the captives who

are in bondage and error in Jesus name,
Amen.

Chapter 4
The Encounter

Let me tell you a little bit, about how I first came to know Jesus and the pull that was always on my heart for Him. I had been in church from the time I was born. The first church I personally remember attending was a small family church that was Holy Ghost filled where they used to speak in tongues. It was hilarious to my brother and me. We would laugh so hard every time the pastor's wife would begin to speak in tongues and each time we would get into major trouble.

During that time, I hated church because it was boring to me. There were very few children there and we had to go to boring children's classes where the teacher was an elderly woman who could hardly keep up with the kids. The only thing I enjoyed and always looked forward to about that class was snack time.

The pastors of that church were beautiful people. They were so caring and loving and most Sundays we went to their house for Sunday Dinner. The pastor's wife was a great cook and she always made plenty of food including desserts. I loved the pastors and enjoyed going to their house but because of my lack of interest in the children's classes, I never learned much.

However, when I was eight years old we started attending a super cool youth oriented church that was fun for everyone. I fell in love with church and I wanted to be there every time the church doors opened. I started to learn about God and I became very inquisitive about who He was and how He related to me.

We had youth classes there and I enjoyed them because I used to hang out, and eat and talk with my friends. It was more like a social club than a class and I loved that. However, when I turned nine years old, something beautiful happened to me. I had gone into the sanctuary to get something from my mother when it happened. The message drew me in. I tried to leave the service and go back to the youth area with my friends but I could not. I sat on the last pew of the church and began to listen to my pastor preach about who Jesus was and I was extremely interested in knowing.

I sat there weeping uncontrollably not really understanding the magnitude of what was happening to me. I just sat there intrigued by this man named Jesus and I wanted to know more; I was hungry for him.

Not long after the message was over, the pastor invited us to come to the altar if we wanted to receive Jesus into our hearts as Lord and Savior.

I did not fully understand what it meant but I was sure that I wanted him in my life. I went to the altar that day without hesitation weeping and wanting to have Jesus. I prayed the prayer of salvation by repeating after the pastor. When it was over, I knew something had happened to me but I just did not know what or how to explain it. I felt different; I knew I would never be the same again. The irony in it all was how the enemy was moving into my life early on to stop the move of Jesus into my life but Jesus was still there presenting himself to me.

Satan was also presenting himself but it was something about Jesus through it all that I knew I needed and I was unwilling to let him go even when I was doing wrong. Jesus began to come alive in me and I began to see things differently concerning salvation and life because of the Word. I continued to follow my mother into the sanctuary to hear the word of God instead of going into the children's ministry to play.

My life would never be the same again after encountering Jesus. I would go on to live a life as best I could for Christ, unfortunately with many flaws and shortcomings. I was not perfect by a long shot and neither can I claim to be today. I have served in the church while still being involved with the things of the world. I have never had a problem with things such as clubbing, drinking, smoking, prostituting or drugs. I was one who enjoyed the company of a man. I spent many Saturday nights entertaining a man and then Sunday morning, entertaining people in the church by singing on the worship team.

I was not pleased with my behavior and I desperately wanted someone to tell me it was not ok to do what I was doing but no one ever addressed my sin. Therefore, I continued to do what I pleased while serving in the church. Pastors, ministers, and leaders, this is not right. You must address sin even at the risk of losing people. Souls should be more important than membership, talents and tithes.

It does not matter if you have the best musician in the world, if he or she is willfully sinning against God without a repentant heart, they cannot continue to serve until they choose to obey God. Please understand; I am not talking about people making mistakes; rather people making a conscious decision to do something that they know is contrary to the Word of God. If your worship leader is sleeping with men in the church and you as the pastor know about it and do nothing; you too are in sin. Eli knew his sons were sinning against God and did nothing and they all were punished.

The Philistines killed his sons and Eli fell over backwards breaking his neck after hearing the news.

The problem with many leaders and pastors is the fact that they are in sin and feel uneasy addressing someone else's sin when they are guilty themselves. I pray that if that is you, that you will turn back to God. Repent of your sin and address the sin in the house of God in order for change to come quickly. It is not too late to get it right. God is a forgiving God; a God of mercy, if he were not, you would already be dead. I pray for every leader now that your hearts will be sensitive to God and that you will turn from wickedness and back to holiness, in Jesus name.

We all have struggles, none of us are perfect. However, we must strive for perfection. I personally fall short of God's glory but He is still unchanging and merciful. He is longsuffering and forgiving. The Lord is the reason that I am alive today. If it were not for Him, I would surely be dead.

Through all the mistakes, shortcoming, and downfalls, I still considered myself a Christian because I never denounced God with my mouth. However, I now know that I had denounced Him in my heart and with my actions repeatedly but His grace and mercy was always there. However, remember grace is not a ticket to sin. I cannot judge anyone because I have been a mess for many years of my life and in some ways, I am still a mess but I can be truthful about it. I have come to grips with the truth. I understand that regardless of my sins, it is never ok to justify it. Sin is sin and we must be truthful about where we are and where we are going.

We cannot ever expect deliverance to come if we do not first desire it and admit that we have a problem. I pray for each of you that you will not try to cover up your sins or to justify your wrongdoing. Be honest and open so that you can be helped. Remember to strive for maturity in Christ and lean on Him when you are weak. Trust God to help you and He will.

I lived many years struggling and in shame because I was living a double life. I was not proud of how I was living or the mistakes I was making but I felt I could not be real and come clean. I wanted to expose myself to get help, but the people in the church were so judgmental. Please do not judge others but pray for them and help them. That is what the church is for, to uphold and uplift one another. The Bible says, "When you see one of your brothers taken in a fault to uphold him and pray for him." Nevertheless, we talk about them and judge them and God is not pleased.

I pray for your deliverance if you are living life unclean. I pray you turn back to

God, surrender your will to the living God, and become whole. I wish someone could have been there for me to tell me what I am telling you, but I could not turn to anyone. Therefore, I went on in my mess, lying, cheating, and fornicating and committing adultery. As you read my story further, you will see how my addiction, a lack of help, and the inability to disclose my struggle kept me in fear, bondage, and sin.

Please do not judge others, pray for them and help them if you can. People are hurting and in need of covenant brothers and sisters to help them stand by upholding and encouraging them. Let us pray for the body of Christ and for those who are lost for their deliverance. I will talk more about my deliverance process as the book progresses and I pray it helps you if you are struggling.

Chapter 5
Ravished

I had known him for a few years before it all happened. I trusted him; he was like a brother to me; that was until I developed a crush on him. It all began innocently. I thought he was beautiful. He was so smart, and talented and handsome and I looked up to him. I yearned to be around him and to spend time talking with him was my delight.

I was in "puppy" love with him. I fell in love with him when I was just ten years old. He was seven years my senior but it did not deter my feelings for him; and by the time I was eleven, I would no longer be a virgin. When he first realized how I felt about him, he thought it was too cute and sweet that I liked him; but that was the extent of it. He did not really show any interest in me at first but it would not be long before he would begin to show much interest in me.

Again, I will not be calling any names because it is not about the individual or what they did but about what Satan was trying to do to destroy me. Even as I tell the story and if you are aware or think, you might be aware, of whom I am referring to, it is not for you to judge or say anything to the person because it is between him, God and me. So please be careful not to involve yourself in this matter.

It all began when I use to spend the night at his house with his baby sister. She and I were great friends at that time and I would often spend the weekends with their family. During that time, he would stare at me with a foreign look in his eyes, which I now know as seduction. He began hugging me often, touching me and paying me sweet compliments.

It was not long before he was fondling me again. Yes, he was the second young man I told you about earlier who fondled me on the bus during a road trip. I believe that is when I first developed feelings for him. However, with age, those feelings seemed to intensify to new heights and I felt love for him instead of just desiring his touch.

He was well aware of my feelings and began to take full advantage of them. I would see him in the hallway and he would pull me into the room where he was and began to touch or kiss me depending on how much time he had before someone might see or miss us.

I must admit it did not bother me or cause me any fear because I was used to being touched and knew him well so I never had any reason to fear he would hurt me. I liked him touching me, I welcomed his kisses but I would have never asked him to penetrate me under any circumstances; I was not ready for anything like that.

However, after months of playing this dangerous game, it would all come to a head one fateful weekend. During this particular weekend, for the first time ever, I became fearful of him because he seemed aggressive with me. He had invited me into his room to listen to CD's and I was excited to do so. CD's were still new at the time and I thought it was cool that he had one of the players. I was fascinated with them as well as with him. Therefore, it was my pleasure to go into his room and listen to CD's. Besides, we had listened to CD's alone in his room before and nothing bad had ever happened. I remember it like it was yesterday; I had gone into his room and he began to play some music. We were singing, playing, laughing, and joking as usual with the door opened and I was having a blast.

However, he got up to change the CD and in the process, he went to close his room door. I was a bit uncomfortable with that and this is how the conversation went from there.

"Hey, what are you doing? Why are you closing the door?"

"Oh I just want us to have a little privacy that's all."

"Uh, could we please not close the door?"

"Why, what's wrong; are you afraid of me?"

"No, it's not that, it's just I would feel better if the door was opened."

"Hey, have I ever hurt you? Have I ever done anything to make you fear me?"

"No!"

"Then why are you afraid, I won't hurt you; ok?"

"OK!"

It was then that he closed the door and locked it. Things continued as before and I was having a blast therefore, my guards were down. However, it did not take long for them to come back up after he began to act strangely.

I remember many things about that day. The sun was shining brightly outside; it was a beautiful spring day. The sheer curtains in his upstairs bedroom allowed the sun to come in and cast light upon the bed. I do not remember what I wore that day except for a long denim skirt because of how it slowly inched up my thighs as he prepared to touch me.

I remember the song that was playing which was "Two Occasions" by the Deele. I also remember being so afraid that I began to tremble as he lifted my skirt and began to touch me. It was different this time. He was more aggressive in his approach of the way touched me. Although I had a bad feeling about it, I tried to relax until he unbuckled his pants and climbed on top of me.

I became extremely nervous, started squirming underneath him, and began pushing him off me. "No I have to go."

"Don't go, I won't hurt you, I promise."

I was too afraid and I was adamant about leaving his room immediately. I stood up from the bed and headed towards the door rather quickly. He grabbed me by the arm and said, "Wait, I won't do anything you don't want me to do, stay."

"I'm sorry, I need to use the restroom; maybe I'll come back later."

After he saw the terror in my eyes and that I was just too afraid to go along with him, he decided to release me. I think if it had been at night or if no one was there, he would have raped me then but he did not.

The rest of the day, he was nice to me. He apologized about what had happened earlier and for making me feel uncomfortable. After that, my guards came falling down and I thought things were back to normal but I was wrong.

All of those things happened on Saturday afternoon and evening. That night I would fall asleep in his sister's room after we stayed up until around 1 am in the morning talking. Around 5 am, he awoke with a gentle shake and a soft whisper.

"Shameka, come here."

"What?"

"Come here."

I was half-asleep, I definitely was not thinking straight and I had totally forgotten what had happened earlier that day that made me afraid. He asked me to come again and I complied. I remember standing up still half asleep and him taking me by my hand leading me down the long dark hallway. His room was directly down the hallway from his sister's room at the very end of the hallway. His mother's room was down stairs situated directly beneath his Sister's room. The third bedroom upstairs was empty as I can recall so no one else was upstairs when he led me to his room except his sister who was fast asleep in her room.

I was fine as he led me down the hallway and still unclear about what was about to transpire. It was not until we arrived in his bedroom that I came to my senses about what his plans were. I was standing at the entrance of his bedroom door when he started pulling me inside the room.

I immediately became afraid and defensive. I was trying to pull away from him but he proved too strong. Once he got me into the room, he closed and locked the door. It was there that he finished what he had started earlier that day. This time I was wearing a nightgown that he easily lifted and he began to touch me. He was holding me affectionately and kissing me.

I began to tremble; he said, "Don't worry I won't hurt you."

I said, "No please stop, I just want to go back to bed" but he insisted that I stay.

He was gentle with me yet very firm. He took me by my hand and pulled mc down to thc floor slowly and gently. He then removed himself from his pajama pants. He moved my underwear to the side and the whole while I was saying, "No, please don't; I'm scared."

He never said another word to me until after it was all over. He just began to kiss and touch me even more passionately. I was trying to be quiet because I was afraid someone would come into the room and see what was happening and I would be embarrassed. I was afraid they would have mistaken the entire scene as a consensual act. I was quietly pleading with him and trying to push him off me but I could not get him off. It was not long before I felt him penetrate me. I began to weep and pray within myself saying, "Lord please help me."

He was raping me but it was as if I was numb. I could not feel a thing although I knew he was inside of me. It is as if God was protecting me from the pain. As I prayed within myself all at once, he just stopped and got off me and pushed himself away from me using his legs as if frightened by something. He began to weep and say, "I'm sorry, I'm sorry, I'm so sorry."

I just wanted to get out of that room as quickly as possible and that is exactly what I did. I got up and went into the bathroom where I sat on the bathroom floor for a few moments crying. I then stood up and looked in the mirror and I was ashamed. I sat on the toilet to use the restroom, when I noticed the blood in my underwear. I removed them, wrapped them in some paper towel, and placed them in the wastebasket.

I then used the restroom, cleaned myself and went back into his sister's room where I tried to go back to sleep. As I lie there unable to sleep, I began thinking to myself that it was my entire fault; I led him on. I should have never allowed him to touch me. I should have never allowed myself to have a crush on a guy that much older than me but now it was too late. I was no longer a virgin and I could do nothing about it.

The positive aspect in the situation is that it never happened again. He never touched me again in that manner and neither did we ever have consensual sex. It was as though he just needed to experience me or "conquer me" and then he was satisfied. He apologized and moved on with his life leaving mine destitute; and he never knew the damage he had inflicted.

He never knew how I went on to become sexually active just a few years later. He never knew that I craved sex as I craved water. He never knew that I needed what he had given me; the attention, the touch, the sex, just to feel loved. He had created a monster along with the others who touched me. It would take years of fighting to overcome the devastating effects of the abuse I had endured.

After the rape, it seemed I became a greater target for older guys and my desire was increasingly towards them.

Chapter 5 Commentary

For many years, I blamed myself for what had happened to me. I thought I deserved rape. After all, I was the one who had a crush on an older guy and I had put myself in that position. I was ashamed of what had happened and therefore, never told a soul until I was 21 years old when I sat down and disclosed many things to my shocked mother who had not known my story at all.

When I revealed to her the rape she was in shock, hurt, and felt bad that she had not been there for me. Although she did not reveal it to me at that time, I would later find out it happened to her also.

It was not until this information surfaced that I began to look at the big picture. From my mother's molestation and rape, to my sister's molestation and becoming sex crazy at a young age; all the way to her daughters being sex crazy and one being brutally raped this painted a clear picture for me.

I began to realize that none of this was coincidence, but targeted. Satan targeted my family. I believe a sexual sin opened the door to him, and he feels he has a right to my bloodline because of it. Refer back to what I previously stated about generational curses in the chapter 2 commentary.

Chapter 6
Dysfunctional

My life drastically changed after the rape in so many ways. I became angry, mean, unforgiving, and hateful. I remember being very callus towards people in general. My bad attitude caused many friends to desert me but I did not know how to cope with the pain. I could not tell anyone what had happened. I felt confused about whether or not it was my fault but either way I looked at it, it was embarrassing, so I did not want to tell anyone.

I was having problems at home, in school with teachers and with peers and I was on the verge of losing it. I remember having to take many trips to the principal's office for defying my teachers, and having verbal fights with my peers. I was mad at the world and the only way I knew to release it was through rebellion.

I developed a horrible attitude. I was extremely defiant and rebellious. I wanted nothing more than to lash out at every boy and man around me in an effort to hurt the man who had hurt me. I did not understand that this was impossible.

I thought it would make me feel better if only I could hurt other men but I was wrong, it made me feel worse. I did not trust a man on any level, whether he was a boyfriend, principal, father figure etc. He was feared instead of trusted. He was in my mind, one that would betray me, hurt me, reject and abandon me.

My father also helped paint this negative picture of men in my mind. After he left us, he would come back to see me over the years until I graduated college periodically. Usually like clockwork, he would appear every other year bearing gifts. The gifts were usually age inappropriate but I was grateful for the effort nonetheless. The things that stood out the most were his new wives from a new city each time I saw him.

My father loved women and was not ashamed to show it. He married women the way he changed clothes and discarded them like day old trash when he was ready for a new one. He made me believe a man was nothing more than an unstable, untrustworthy convenience that was needed, but only good for a moment and must be released. I felt afraid of another man doing to me that which my father had done to my mother and countless other women. Although I loved him, I felt so much anger towards him for abandoning me.

I was in middle school now, and life for me became more difficult and confusing. I had major self-esteem issues that were weighing me down already but the incidence I am about to share with you caused that low self-esteem to manifest even further.

I had an older sister who was about seven years older than I was. When I was around twelve, she was about nineteen when we had a horrible fight, which ended badly. Before I explain what happened that day let me say this. My sister and I never really got along. She for whatever reason did not like me and made it known to me whenever possible. Now remember my mother had six children by her first husband and then me (her seventh child) by her second husband.

My sister often teased me and made me feel different, and less important. She used to say things to me like, "You are not really a part of this family; we adopted you." She would say, "Momma found you in a trashcan and decided to raise you." Her words affected me deeply and hurt me tremendously as she would taunt me constantly.

She often did things to torment me including hurting me physically. She would burn me purposely with the straightening comb on my ears whenever she would do my hair; and when I would run away from her after burning me, she would send my brother to catch me and bring me back. She was mean to me and I hated it; because I loved her and wanted to have a sisterly relationship with her but she would not allow me to.

We would argue over the smallest things especially concerning my personal belongings. My mother would buy me things like deodorant, perfume; hair gel etc. and I would try to hide them from her because she had a habit of taking my things and using them up from me. She used to allow her friends to wear my clothes or give them away. I would get so angry because I had asked her repeatedly not to bother my things, but she never listened to me.

We would argue over the phone, TV, it did not matter how small something was it was always big between us. This particular day that the fight occurred, started out normal. It was summertime and I had gone outside to play with friends. A friend of mine had come home with me to get some water because we were tired and thirsty. When I entered into the house, my sister picked a fight with me.

The argument escalated and I was preparing to leave the house. I went into my mother's room to get something before leaving when my sister just attacked me. She bit me on my breast like an animal and pulled a patch of my hair out. I managed to get away from her by fighting and kicking as best I could but she soon caught up to me in the hallway of our house, near the kitchen. My sister was not only older but a lot bigger than I was. I was small and did not weigh much at the time. I had not had to fight anyone of her strength and speed before and it proved too much for me.

She grabbed me by my hair again and tried to drag me into the kitchen, but I was holding on to the doorpost of the kitchen for dear life after hearing her intentions for taking me into the kitchen. As she pulled me with all of her might, she chanted, "I hate you, I'm going to kill you.

I regret to say this, but if it were not for the grace of God and an angel protecting me that day, I believe she would have tragically killed me. After she could not get me into the kitchen, she dragged me into our den where we had a trophy case over the bar. She managed to grab a vase from the glass case and began beating me with it in the top of my head.

She left cuts in the top of my head and a scar on the side of my face for life. She also managed to hit me in the mouth with the vase using an uppercut motion breaking my front tooth in half. Scarred mentally and physically from the beating, I struggled to forgive her.

I hated her for what she had done to me. It took me years to forgive her although she tried constantly to win my affection. I know you are probably wondering how could my own sister do such a thing; well to this day I do not have an answer for that, other than Satan was trying to kill me and he used my own sister to do it.

My sister had two small children at the time and they witnessed the entire incident. Although I did not press charges against her, she went to jail nonetheless. I was a minor, so the state pressed charges against her. I had to go to school with a chipped tooth and that was so embarrassing.

My friends teased me and made me feel ugly. I was hurt, angry, and too embarrassed to tell anyone what my sister had done to me. I lied about how it happened to keep from feeling more ashamed then I already felt. It was horrible, and affected also was my self-esteem because of the taunting and name calling being inflicted on me; kids were mean and never had mercy on anyone. If you had a flaw, they were going to speak of it until they had gotten enough of it, which was usually never.

I endured so many painful occurrences, not only at school, but in my home as well. It was not easy growing up in my household with all the constant fighting and bickering that took place daily. I was a nervous wreck every time someone would start to argue because it usually turned into a knock down drag out fight where someone would get hurt.

I witnessed so many hurtful things under that roof until I would need an entire book to disclose it. I cannot tell it all, but I can give you some examples of what I lived through. I saw one of my brothers choke another one of my brothers until he was shaking and his eyes were rolling back in his head and almost unconscious when I ran to get my mother who intervened just in time.

I saw one of my brothers beat another one of my brothers with his fists until he was screaming and begging him to stop. When the beating was over my brother, who had been beat threw bricks and bottles at my other brother's head trying to kill him. I saw one of my brothers grab a knife to stab another one of my brothers with it while they were in the heat of an argument. I saw my mother step between them and the knife because she was so tired that she did not care if she died. Death seemed more desirable to her at that time.

I saw one of my brothers hit one of my sisters in her eye so hard, it swelled her eye up twice its size. I watched her grab a knife and chase him down the street with it trying to kill him. I saw one of my brothers grab a thick iron bar from our front door to hit another one of my brothers in the head with it when I cried out with a loud shout. "Please don't, you will kill him." I thank God my words stopped him before it was too late.

I could go on and on about what I witnessed behind closed doors in my home but I think you get the picture. It was pure hell for me. I had perfect attendance in school every year not because I loved school so much but because it was a break from the constant fighting in my home amongst my siblings. Worn out from the turmoil in our home were my mother and me.

I have the sweetest mother that ever walked the face of the earth, in my opinion, and it broke my heart to have to watch my mother suffer through this with her children day in and out. My mother was a woman of great sacrifice and love. She was the best example of a strong black woman to me. She was patient, loving, kind, forgiving, encouraging, prayerful, and supportive. That is why it tore me up to see the pain in her eyes concerning her children. Much of the fighting occurred when my mother was away at work and trying to provide for her seven children as a single mom. It was sad that she always received bad news that something awful had happened again at home.

I must admit, things became increasingly better in my family the older my siblings and I got. We developed a strong family bond and tradition that would endure for many years. We had Sunday dinner every week at my mother's house or special outings together as a family. We had so much fun during those times. We always had each other's back. Even if we fought, we never allowed anyone else to fight us. We loved one another and it truly showed after we learned the value of family and the importance of togetherness. I love all of my siblings and I appreciate each one for what they bring to my life.

Life for me was not easy and I almost ran away from home because I was tired of the pain. The streets would have eaten me alive and I am sure with the sexual experiences I had already encountered, in combination with my low self-esteem, I would have become a prostitute to survive. I would have been an easy mark for a pimp no doubt. I thank God for not allowing that to happen to me. God was so faithful to preserve me in the midst of all of the pain.

I am also grateful that I no longer struggle with low self-esteem, and that I know my worth. I am not seeking love or acceptance from people anymore but rather from God. I love the peace and joy God has provided me as I began to trust him and seek for love in him. No greater love I know than His.

Chapter 6 Commentary

I recently heard a pastor say that generational curses are not relevant to Christians today. I agree in some ways but not in the way, I believe he meant it. I do believe that if we are in Christ, we are now under grace. Therefore, we do not have to accept those curses as our own. However, a curse passed down through the generational line, must be broken in order not to affect the family member who is now under grace.

When I look at my family and what we endured in our household, I can easily say without any doubt in my mind that it was abnormal for family to fight in this manner. Please understand, that what happened with my brothers and sisters happened with their father's sisters and brothers.

My mother, shocked by the fighting she witnessed could not believe it. She had thirteen siblings yet never witnessed any such fighting in her home. She was amazed that children would talk back to their parents because that was unheard of in her home. In addition, her brothers and sisters had disagreements but they had never fought like animals in resolving their issues.

Now think about it, my six older siblings were all involved in fighting one another. I was the only one who did not get involved with the fighting. However, my siblings came from that same bloodline in which fighting was the norm. My father's family was different. They did not fight one another in this manner.

So you cannot tell me that generational curses do not exist or that they are not relevant even among Christians because if you do not know that you have been liberated you will continue to walk as one in bondage. I have seen it repeatedly in so many situations. People are a product of their environments, bloodlines, and family history.

Breast cancer and diabetes passed down from one generation to another has been documented and likewise addictive behaviors such as alcoholism and sexual addictions etc. passes down. I am not saying one has to accept it and say, "Well momma had diabetes so I guess I will too. No, we can cover ourselves under the blood of Jesus and denounce these things. We can pray for the forgiveness of the sins of our fathers. Pray that we are no longer indebted to the consequences of those sins.

Prayer:

I pray for your deliverance if you are struggling with some type of generational curse in Jesus name. I pray that you would find peace in the Lord and restoration by his power. Lord God; do it for them even now Jesus as I pray it. Break the bands of wickedness, the chains of sin and heal them of their disease. Show them your love and mercy and be gracious to them oh God that they too may experience the freedom you have given me in your darling son, Jesus' name, Amen.

Chapter 7
My Desire

After the rape, things were quiet for a while. However, it was not long before things began to heat up again. It was as if I had become a magnet because men who were significantly older than I was, began to have an interest in me. It started with a well-known singer who often frequented our church. He would always tell me how pretty I was and how much he wanted to be with me.

He began to take me on the side of the church where we would lean up against the wall and he put his hands under my clothes and fondle me; and I loved every moment of it. This is so embarrassing to me and I thought I would never tell a soul. However, as I look back I see a broken little girl looking for love in a messed up world.

As I stated before, we often went on trips with the church or Sister Churches and or our Bishop would come down to minister at our church. I met the Bishop's Armor bearer (Assistant) a short while after the rape had occurred. The first time we laid eyes on each other something magical happened. I promise you to this day, I do not understand how or why we had such an attraction to one another but it was immediately evident.

He had to be at least 12 years my senior. He was tall and handsome and very well behaved in front of the Bishop. The first time we were alone, it took him no time at all to begin fondling me as often as time would allow. This man had a hold on my body and my young mind. It was something about him that was so magnetic and intriguing; I loved to be near him. The fondling happened literally, every time I saw him regardless of the city. It happened in Dallas, South Carolina, Detroit, Alabama and Mississippi. This went on for quite some time until we left the ministry.

I saw him a couple of years later at a funeral and he fondled me that day as well behind a church van in the parking lot of the church. We had such a weird attraction to one another. We never spoke a word. When we would see each other it was automatic, we would find a place to be alone, and we would kiss, hug and he would touch me.

We never had intercourse and that was a blessing. God was protecting me because he tried to come into a room and have sex with me in Detroit but my roommates came back right when he was about to undress me. All praise is due to God because I was terrified. I was still very afraid of sex and did not want it but I had to be touched; I needed it.

I was addicted to the feeling of a man's hand caressing, rubbing and fondling me but that was the extent of my desire and my high until high school.

Older men chased me constantly and many of them touched me inappropriately because I was in love with being touched. I welcomed it completely; I longed for it. I am very embarrassed to say this but I never resisted the touch of any man that I found attractive regardless of his age or how long I had known him until I was older and wiser. I guess I had a little sense back then because at least the man had to be attractive before he could have the privilege of touching me.

It is clear to see that I had some deep-rooted issues. I was dealing with a classic case of low self-esteem, insecurity and the need to feel loved. I believe this all stemmed from several factors. One factor being the low self-esteem and insecurity of my mother and other women of my family, which passed down to me. Another factor, which I believe caused my behavior, was the abandonment of my father and the root of rejection planted and growing within me.

I was in search of love and acceptance and I felt loved in those moments, which were perverted to say the least. I thank God that He has healed and delivered me from low self-esteem and insecurity and I no longer need the affirmation of anyone except Him to be happy.

Chapter 7 Commentary

    This chapter is a prime example of how sexual sins pass down from one generation to the next. Let me reiterate that I believe there are sinful sexual rituals that have occurred somewhere in my generational line that have caused the enemy to believe he has a right to me.

    I was ignorant to this for many years and lived in sexual bondage thinking there was not a way to escape it. Honestly, I did not want to escape it for myself; but I was tired of displeasing God and knew I had to. Otherwise, I would still be out there on a daily basis binging on great sex and that is the truth from my heart. Sex is fun, it feels good, and who would not want to have it? I choose not to have it because I love God with my whole heart. If I did not, I would not restrain from experiencing one of the best feelings in the world.

    The flesh enjoys things that feel good to it, even when it is bad for it. After I could not have sex, I began to gain weight rapidly because I ate to fill my sexual void. Now I am struggling to overcome a food addiction. We have to be careful not to move from one addiction to another when ridding ourselves of bad habits.

I am so grateful God has revealed the truth to me and that I can live free from sin with His help. The key to overcoming any addiction is being aware that you have a problem and seeking out the appropriate solution. I am currently seeking out the appropriate solution to this food addiction and being careful not to return to sex to substitute it.

I am not one who enjoys any other highs. I do not drink or smoke so that is not an option. Anger is the only other high I have ever experienced. Although some may disagree with ne, anger is definitely addictive. In my case, I enjoyed the feeling of power I got from being angry.

When angry, I am bold, careless, daring and upfront. I never bite my tongue when angry and I feel in control of everything around me. The problem with that, as with other addictive behaviors, is that it has negative repercussions in the end. Anything we do in our lives that is unhealthy and unbalanced will result in negative outcomes. Nothing good ever comes from something done outside of moderation. It is possible to overcome generational curses or strongholds through prayer and other factors.

To overcome generational strongholds, we must denounce any ties we have had with the sinful acts that were associated with evil and Godless practices that keep us in bondage. We must pray for forgiveness of the sins of our fathers and ask God to break every curse of the generations. This is the only way to be free of curses passed down from one generation to another.

I pray even now that every generational curse passed down to whoever reads this book, will receive healing and deliverance will come forth in the name of Jesus. We are free from every curse and sin of our fathers and we walk in the liberty of Christ.

Jesus has freed us from the laws of sin and death and a negative inheritance. We are now walking according to what God has purposed and not according to what the enemy has plotted against us or according to what we deserve because of our sins in Jesus name, I pray Amen.

Our lives are affected in so many ways by what we experience from our childhood on. Those negative experiences do not simply go away, but they manifest repeatedly in our adult lives in many different situations, until healing comes from our past.

My past affected my decision-making, my thought processes, attitudes, and beliefs about myself. I made terrible decisions based on the painful things I endured that caused me to see myself as bad, unworthy, unlovable, and undesirable. I thought the only way I would experience love was through sex because nothing else about me was worth anything.

I was wrong and I wish I could have made better decisions but it is ok. God is my healer and my worth; I have found my esteem in Him. He is the reason for my transformation and mind renewal. I am forever indebted to Him for saving my life from complete destruction. If it had not been for Him I do not even want to think about where I would be. Thank you father for your redeeming quality and generous mercy; I am eternally grateful.

Chapter 8
Ready for Love

I was now in high school and my attraction to older men continued. I was a freshman in high school and interested in senior boys only. I could tell you many stories about this but I will not. I am going to get to my point rather quickly.

After fearing sex since the rape, I had not been willing to do it. However, I was now officially dating an older guy who was very kind, sweet and gentle. He was my first real relationship and he was special to me. He was the man to whom I gave my virginity. Although already taken, he was the one I willingly gave my virginity. I remember how it all happened the first time.

He was so sweet to me; he did not try to force himself on me at all. I remember for months at a time I had told him I was not ready for sex and he never once complained. One day while being intimate, I decided I was ready. I remember it like it was yesterday. The conversation went like this.

"Baby, I'm ready."

"What, are you sure?"

"Yes, I'm scared but I'm sure."

"Baby you are shaking."

"I know because I'm really scared."

"Baby we don't have to do it. I'll still love you."

That brought so much comfort to my heart and it made me want to do it even more. I responded, "Baby I want to."

"Alright baby, I promise I will be gentle."

"Ok, please baby, don't hurt me."

"I won't"

Then it happened; he was so gentle and loving and I was in heaven. This experience was beautiful, perfect, and just as I had been addicted to the touch of a man; now I would become addicted to sex.

My boyfriend and I had sex constantly. Whenever there was time and opportunity, we were being intimate. I was a sex junkie; I loved everything about it, it gave me a rush. I wanted it morning, noon, and night but only with him. One thing I can say about me, I never wanted sex with multiple partners. I was really into whomever I was with at the time.

We broke up a year and a half later because I made an awful mistake. Before dating him I was, intrigued by another senior at our high school that I literally waited on. That is why initially, I would not accept my boyfriend's pursuit because I was waiting on my crush. He was in a relationship but I wanted him badly enough to wait for him. However, he seemed happy with his current girlfriend and I became tired of waiting and moved on to my boyfriend.

It was not until he graduated and came back and saw me at a football game where I was cheering that he showed interest in me. I quickly forgot that I had a boyfriend for a moment because I was so excited that he had finally come for me. I had told my best friend the year before that he was going to be mine and my opportunity had come.

That night I would kiss him and he placed a hickey on my neck unknowingly because he did it so smoothly and I was wrapped up in him I hadn't noticed. When I went into my best friend's house, she saw it and said girl you are going to get in trouble. I could not believe it. I was so angry that he had done that; I iced it down trying to get rid of it but it did not go away. My boyfriend's best friend told him about the hickey and he came home from school to confront me.

I was so upset and hurt that he had told him because I did not want to lose him. I told him the truth about what had happened and it infuriated him. I broke up with him, not because I did not want him anymore but I felt he would never be able to trust me again. A mistake I regretted for years. I wanted to go back to him many times but was afraid he would shoot me down and I was afraid of rejection.

Funny thing is, I found out some years later he wanted me just as much and would be alone for several years before even attempting another relationship. For a moment, I thought he and I were going to get back together and perhaps be married but I was wrong. Too many years had lapsed and too many hurtful experiences on both our parts would not allow our union.

I soon became involved with another older guy after experiencing a few casual dating experiences. Let me re-iterate that I am not proud of any of my behavior that went contrary to God, sexual or otherwise. This is not to glorify any of those things but to shed light on Satan's plot to destroy us through bad decisions and disobedience to God. I had some meaningless sexual encounters during this period that were awful for me and I hated every moment of what I was doing, but I felt helpless in my need to feed my desires for sex and love.

I told you I felt like an addict; it was as if I had to have that feeling to feel loved; or to just to feel alive. It was awful and the number of men that took advantage of my ignorance, low self-esteem and need to feel loved, embarrasses me but I cannot do anything about it. If I could rewind the time, I would but I cannot.

Therefore, since I cannot, I chose to forgive myself, those who took advantage of me, those who hurt me, and I have moved on with my life to live at peace. I do not hold anything in my heart against anyone. I even forgave God whom I was greatly angry with because I felt he allowed those things to happen to me when he could have stopped it. However, I came to understand that it was all for a reason.

God is not the author of confusion; He is the prince of peace. He does not inflict bad things upon us, Satan does but God allows it when He can use it for His glory and our making. Therefore, we must trust God that anything he has allowed us to go through is for a good reason. I know it is difficult to accept some things happening to us and we can become bitter easily. I was bitter for a while concerning the rape.

I was angry concerning the abandonment of my father and I blamed God for not being there for me. It was not His fault; I know that now and I thank Him for keeping me safe in the midst of all that I endured. My point is, if you are angry with God because you feel He was not there for you, rethink your stance and seek God for clarity on why He allowed it. I promise you will find peace and comfort in knowing He was there all along.

I thank God that I soon found a man that I would settle down with for several years. I will tell you about that relationship shortly but first let us talk about another short-lived relationship that was devastating and almost cost me my life.

Chapter 9
Liar, Cheater, Stalker

Although he was much older than I was, I did not have a clue. He had lied about his age and told me he was 21 years old but in fact, he was 27 years old. I would find that out sometime later during our relationship after finding his birth certificate on the floor of his apartment. I was living a dangerous life and the sad part about it; my mother was unaware of it. I will talk about that more a bit later as well.

The man I had become involved with was very experienced. He was very different from the high school senior in which I had been involved. He taught me things about sex I did not know, and did things to me I had not experienced. It was incredible. It was like taking a stronger version of a drug and feeling a different effect on your body. He made me feel incredible the way he touched me and held me. I was in awe of his skills and knowledge.

He had his own apartment and I was going there as often as possible. My mother was clueless. She thought I was staying at my best friend's house; when in fact, I would leave her house and go to his house and spend the night. It was not long before this relationship took a turn for the worse.

I soon realized he was a liar, and a cheater. He took advantage of my ignorance. He was with other women often but he was such a master liar that whatever he told me about the situation, I believed it. There were several times when I knew within myself he was lying but I just dealt with it because I did not want to lose him; he was like a drug to me.

It was not until I found his birth certificate and confronted him about his age, when I realized I no longer wanted to be with him because this was too much for me to handle. I will leave out many details but let's just say all hell broke loose when I tried to break it off with him.

That night in particular, he held me hostage; raped me repeatedly, mentally abused me and physically bruised me. The following morning when he decided to release me, it was not without a fight. It was the first time I would be hit by a man. As I walked out of the front door, and headed down the stairwell, he snatched my purse and set it at the top of the stairs. He then sat down on the stair beneath it to block me from getting to my purse.

Each time I reached to get it, he would push me backwards. I could have fallen down the stairs but I held onto to the guardrail to keep my balance. He played a game of cat and mouse with me for a while until I became frustrated and fought back. I told him if he pushed me again, I was going to slap him; he pushed me and I did as I had promised.

That was a huge mistake. The next thing I remember is fists being thrown, and landing upside my head. If it were not for his neighbor who intervened, I do not know what would have happened. I was able to get away from him that day because of the kindness of that stranger. However, he stalked me for the next several months after the incidence.

I remember a time when I was staying at my best friend's house when I received a call unexpectedly from him saying he loved the black dress I was wearing. That freaked me out knowing he was watching me and I had not seen him. Another time, we were having a girl's night where we were sleeping over at my best friend's house. We ordered pizza and began watching movies. When the pizza arrived, he called and told me that he wanted some pizza also; I dropped the phone in terror. I was so afraid of him. He kept popping up unexpectedly in places and calling me and letting me know he had been following or watching me.

I wanted to tell my mother but what was I going to say; she did not know about this man. I wanted to tell my brothers but I was afraid they were going to kill him, and then me for being with him. I could not do anything. There were a lot of incidences and horrible confrontations I had with him but the one I am about to disclose was the worst one in which I thought I was going to die.

I was downtown Dallas at McDonalds waiting on the bus to arrive. I was with a friend girl and we decided to get something to eat while we waited on the bus. While sitting at the table, she saw him enter the location. She said, "Don't look back and don't panic but he is here. I don't think he saw you so let's go into the restroom and wait until he leaves and we will catch the next bus."

I agreed and we slowly and quietly went into the rest room. I held my head down following closely to her on the opposite side where he could not see me. We waited for about twenty minutes in the restroom. She then decided to go and check to see if he was gone before I would come out. As soon as she opened the door, he was standing at the door waiting. I saw him and my eyes locked with his as I trembled in fear.

He calmly said to me, "Hi, come here, I need to talk to you." I did not want to go but I knew I did not have a choice. I followed him to a table where he began to question me. He said, "I know you have a new man, who is this fella?"

"That is none of your business; can we talk about something else, please?"

"No, I want to talk about this dude you left me for!" His voice would be calm and then it would escalate eerily in and out during our conversation. His posture, demeanor and even how he looked at me sent chills through my body. I had a bad feeling about the entire scene and all I could do was pray within me that I would leave there alive.

It was not long before things began to go terribly wrong. He reached across the table for my hands and held them tightly as he began asking questions. When I would say something he did not like, he would squeeze my hands roughly and say, "Let's try that again."

I squirmed anxiously hoping the entire while by some miracle I would soon wake up unharmed in my bed. However, this was no dream and he went on to ask me, "Have you kissed your new boyfriend?"

I answered, "Yes."

He laughed and leaned across the table and said, "Kiss me the way you kissed him."

Refusing to kiss him, he yanked me by my hands towards him and repeated himself more forcefully, "I said kiss me the way you kissed that dude." I did as he asked and kissed him softly on his lips.

He yelled, "No, kiss me the way you kissed that nigga!" I jumped nervously, leaned in, and kissed him once again this time with more passion. My friend who was now impatient, began pacing near our table, and said to him, "Leave her alone, she doesn't want you anymore!"

He cursed her out and told her, "You don't know me; I will cut your throat before you can utter another word to me." He then turned towards me and said, "You better tell your girl to get on before I…"

"Please just go, I'll be ok. Just wait for me outside." She stood there not wanting to leave me alone with him. I looked her in the eyes and said, "Please." She walked away and sat at a table on the other side of the restaurant where she could see me clearly.

After a while, he said, "Come and walk with me."

I thought to myself, "Lord this man is going to kill me if I leave out of this restaurant." I was afraid to go outside with him but he did not leave me much of a choice.

He took me by my arm pulling me from the booth and forced me outside. I was resisting him as he began to take me around on the side of the building where there was hardly any traffic and a big dumpster. I was trying so hard to keep him from taking me there until my feet were dragging on the concrete as he pulled me like a ragdoll. My friend followed us and stood at the corner watching.

He looked into my eyes, grabbed me by my throat, slammed me up against the wall, and said, "If I can't have you, nobody can."

My friend ran up on him and began to yell at him, "Leave her alone" as I stood there helpless with tears pouring from my eyes. He took out a huge switchblade from his front pant pocket, opened it, lunged towards her while still holding on to my neck, and said, "If you do not leave, I will kill you first." She stumbled backwards almost losing her balance before she took out running and yelling out to me that she was going for help.

He then tightened his grip around my neck almost picking me up off the ground as he choked me. With a look of pure evil in his eyes as if he was possessed, he looked into my eyes and said, "I should kill you right now. Tell me you love me or I will."

He released his grip so I could say it. I coughed a few times and swallowed deeply and managed a fearful, "I love you."

He whispered sweetly without a hint of anger in his voice, "Now kiss me again and tell me you love me."

Trembling and confused, I did as he said. We kissed for a short while passionately before he suddenly pulled away and began speaking incoherently and then ranting, crying, and saying, "I love you, see what you made me do, I love you. The knife was still wavering in his hand near my face as he continued his ranting. I want to make love to you so bad right now; all I want is to hold you and love you like I use to but you took that from me. Why baby, why are you are giving somebody else my love? I love you, I need you."

I could not answer; all I could do was cry. He placed the knife up to my neck once again as tears streamed down his face and he angrily said with his teeth clenched, "I won't let you go; he can't have you either."

I knew this was it; I saw my young life flash before my eyes. I saw my mother crying for the loss of her baby girl. I heard the stories of loved ones ringing out above my casket. I closed my eyes and prayed silently, "Lord please forgive me of all of my sins so I can see you; don't let me suffer, please let me die quickly." I stood still anticipating deaths arrival when suddenly he released his grip and the tip of the knife was no longer pressing against the vein in my neck. I opened my eyes hesitantly and watched him as he backed away from me with a solemn look on his face and said, "Just go." I was so relieved but nervous at the same time thinking he was going to stab me in my back as I walked away but I took that chance.

He followed me but he did not harm me. God was truly with me and He preserved my life. After this, I finally told my boyfriend what was going on. It was not until he intervened that the stalking and constant threats stopped. My boyfriend, his brother and cousin all went to pay him a visit and after that, I never saw or heard from him again.

Although some years later, I found out, he was dating another young girl, which was my best friend's cousin. I told her he was crazy and her cousin needed to leave him but it was too late. He stabbed her during an altercation; thank God, she survived it. That could have been me; this is proof that God saved my life that day.

Chapter 9 Commentary

What I experienced at the hands of my stalker I believe was to escalate the process of what the enemy had plotted against me. Actually, it was the enemies plan to take my life and it would almost happen at the hands of this chosen vessel by Satan to kill me.

This particular man had every intention on slicing my throat the day he held a huge blade to my neck and threatened to kill me. I was terrified but it was the mercy of God and the angels of the Lord that saved me that day, I am one hundred percent sure of it.

I believe although he did not kill me physically; something in me spiritually had died. I became more sexually inclined after this experience like never before and I believe it was because of the spirits this man carried. He was an avid sex fiend. Sex was mostly what he spoke about and what we did constantly. If he could have, he would have had sex for breakfast lunch, dinner, and desserts too. I believe that is why he dated so many women so that he could obtain sex at the drop of a dime.

Ms. Shameka Bonner

I was blessed to make it out of that situation alive and I was equally blessed to have gotten out of the relationship when I did because I believe I would have ended up an absolute nymphomaniac had I stayed. Thank God for His mercy!

Chapter 10

Aborted

I was now a sophomore in high school and my boyfriend was in college at Grambling State. He was the sweetest man that ever lived; and I still believe that to this very day. We would be together over the next five years of my life. The first year was glorious. It wasn't until I got pregnant that things between us changed.

The reason the pregnancy changed everything was because we had a scare early on in our relationship and he was well aware that I was not at all interested in having a baby. I was afraid and adamant about not having a child while I was still in high school. We were in love and I was sure we would be married someday. After marriage, I would have been more than willing to have his babies but not at that time.

We had a long talk, I cried and expressed my inner most fears and begged of him to be very careful not to get me pregnant. In addition, for a while, he seemed to respect that. However, he had become insecure concerning our relationship. I tried to reassure him that he was my choice and that I had no plans of ever leaving. However, his fears of me leaving had gotten the best of him and caused him to do the unthinkable.

He had come home from school and we were intimate. It was during that time that he violated me. My sweet loving boyfriend took the liberty of holding me down and purposely ejaculating inside of me to get me pregnant. I knew instantly that I was pregnant without any doubt in my mind.

I cried at that very moment because I was sure that I was pregnant. He said to me, "Stop crying, you're not pregnant. It is going to be ok."

I continued to cry as he walked out of my front door, got into the car with his friend, and left me there crying, broken, hurting and pregnant. Just as I had suspected, I was indeed pregnant. I would miss my cycle by two days and I called him immediately.

He said, "You're just two days late, that doesn't mean you're pregnant."

"I'm never late; I'm pregnant I just know it."

I was right, a few days later my breasts became extremely sore and I began to have morning sickness. During that time, my mother began to notice that something was not right. I remember one morning throwing up and she looked at me strangely and said, "Girl I hope you are not pregnant."

I said, "Momma, I'm not pregnant, I just had some cold in my throat that I was trying to bring up and it made me feel sick."

"Well I hope you are right because that is that same nasty yellow stuff I used to throw up when I was pregnant."

"Momma, I'm not pregnant!"

"Well why is your skin looking so pretty? It is glowing."

"I don't know, it's probably because of my new face cream; but I'm not pregnant."

I knew in my heart I was but I could not bring myself to tell my mother that. She loved and trusted me and I did not want to disappoint her.

My boyfriend came home that weekend, I took a home pregnancy test, and it came back positive. I was so pissed off at him I did not know what to do. I felt like I hated him; he knew how much I did not want to have a baby at that time but there I was sixteen and pregnant.

I was so upset and determined not to have his baby after how he gotten me pregnant. I just knew I would conceive my first baby during passionate lovemaking. I wanted my first-born and every child for that matter to be a love child not a child born out of violation.

I told him that I could not have the child. I explained to him that it would kill my mother if she found out I was pregnant. I will talk more about my mother in the chapter commentary. Well of course, he did not agree with me, but I did not care what he thought. I was not going to have the baby. Our relationship went from being beautiful to absolutely awful. I hated him and I showed him constantly.

After I had threatened him several times and showed my blatant disrespect and anger for him, he finally agreed to my terms. He made an appointment for me to get the abortion along with his mother's help. I was so scared but excited to get it done and over with. I was not about to be a teenage mother.

The day of the appointment, we went in and immediately I had to talk to someone about my decision. Then they took me in a room and I had to watch a video. After the video, I asked when they were going to perform the actual abortion and she advised me that they did not do abortions there. She stated that they were a counseling center aimed to prevent abortion. I was livid.

I walked out of that room screaming for my boyfriend. When I got to him, I was spitting and crying while screaming at him and hitting him with all of my might. I was angry that he was still trying to persuade me not to have the abortion. We fought all the way home and I wanted to kill him.

During this same time, I was grieving over the loss of my brother. His funeral and my abortion all happened in the same week. I was so broken and angry; I wanted my brother back, and my body back without a child in it. I wanted to tell my mother so badly, about what I was going through because she was my best friend. I told her everything except about anything that had to do with sex. She was too distraught to handle anything else at that time because she was having the most difficult time with my brother's death.

Therefore, it would finally happen; I had the abortion a day before my brother's funeral. I was not saddened back then by the abortion nor did I have any feelings towards having it because of the circumstances. I just wanted that baby out of me; I wanted to erase what my boyfriend had done to me. I thought that it would also erase the memory but it had not.

We would go on in our rocky relationship for the next several years. The only reason why I had not left him was that I wanted to pay him back every day for what he had done to me. I treated him like dirt. I called him names, I hit on him, I degraded and humiliated him every chance I got.

He felt so guilty about what he had done that he would just take it. He would do anything I said including drop out of school to stay home and work and take care of me. I was so angry, hateful and mean to him. I stole three and half years of his life because he was miserable. The crazy thing was he was miserable with me because I made sure of it but when I finally broke up with him, he was miserable without me.

He had a very difficult time overcoming us. He begged me to stay but I told him I just did not love him anymore. The man I had loved with a crazy love, whom I knew I would eventually marry, became my enemy and the target of my hate. I would later go on to forgive him and we were able to become friends again. I love him like a brother and if he ever needed me, I would be there.

Chapter 10 Commentary

I believe that when a person has a sex demon it also comes with a murderous spirit. I was having sex on a consistent basis unless there was no time or opportunity to do so. Sex was always on my mind or I was actually in the act of it; it engulfed me. I was not only a sex fiend but now I was a murderer also.

I had become a murderer unaware. In my heart, because of anger and disappointment, I felt the child must die because I refused to allow a child to live conceived during an act of sex that violated me.

The rape I endured caused the incidence with my boyfriend to make me feel equally violated or raped again by the outright disregard of my thoughts, feelings, and emotions. I thought if he did not care about my feelings, why should I care about his.

I came to a point of trying to punish him through destroying an innocent child. Can you see the cycle of destruction in that? I was an innocent child who had my innocence stolen and now I had taken the life of my innocent child.

I will discuss the murderous spirit that was operating in me more in a future chapter, but I will leave you with this for now. I would go on for years feeling no affects of my decision to abort my child. However, the time would come when it would engulf me with sadness as I thought back to what I had done to my precious baby.

Chapter 11

Transition

After I had broken up with my boyfriend of five years, I began considering making a commitment to my relationship with Christ. Unbelievably, everything you have read concerning my life thus far all happened while I was actively involved in the church or attending on a regular basis.

I was living a double life and I hated it, but I had some serious issues that I did not know how to remedy. Although I knew, what I was doing was wrong; I never once desired to be away from God or His presence. I prayed often, went to church whenever the doors opened, but I had a problem; I loved sex.

I remember often wishing that sex was not a sin because I felt if I could just be saved and have sex freely; I would be the perfect Christian. That is laughable when I think about it today considering all the other issues I had. However, I struggled in making a definite commitment to God because I knew I would have to give up sex and I just was not ready for that. Remember it was like an addiction for me; I craved it.

After being in committed relationships all through high school, I was tired of being committed. I felt like I was missing something so I reneged on my consideration of being committed to Christ or anyone. I recall going through a crazy phase for six whole months that felt like decades.

I refuse to disclose exactly what I did but I will say this, I dated several guys at the same time, with each of them knowing that we were not exclusive. Although I made some bad choices during that time, I am proud to say that I did not sleep with all of them. However, I made enough bad decisions that I am too embarrassed to speak of, which caused me to change lanes quickly and head in a different direction.

I had finally decided to make that change and become committed to God fully. What I experienced over the next year was incredible. I became so involved with prayer and bible study that my life was changing rapidly right before my eyes. I recall having special supernatural experiences that changed my entire outlook on who Jesus was and Christianity. Life was so good!

I was living on my college campus during this time when I decided to make this change. I gave up my life of partying, romp shaking and sex. All of these things had been in competition with going to church and my relationship with Christ. I had to let them go in order to move forward. My friends were not so thrilled with my decision and many of them would no longer call me friend.

I had to live with the rejection and abandonment but I felt secure in knowing I had the greatest friend of all, which was Jesus. However, others benefited from my change and my relationship with God. God was using me to speak life into others and help them come to know Him. I was not ashamed of the gospel of Christ and became known among the fellas as church girl.

It was not an endearing name but one chosen to taunt me because I was not playing their game. It was all good; I took it as a compliment. During that time, God truly taught me many spiritual truths.   It was a beautiful time and I love it.

Chapter 12
Fallen

Motivated by the word to be better and to see others better, I was spending a lot of quality time in the presence of God and in His Word. I was learning so much and growing rapidly. God had really begun to deal with me in dreams, visions, and prophesy.

I began to have great spiritual encounters with God that were mind-blowing and incredibly fascinating. I was so into the word that I began a bible study on campus and became somewhat of a mentor to my friends and associates.

I was doing great; my future looked promising and I thought I was no longer able to fall victim to acts of fornication. I loved God with my whole heart and I wanted nothing more than to please him. He was my life, joy and peace; I needed him like the air I breathed.

I would soon realize my efforts to deliver and heal myself were like patching a busted tire; it was only temporary. I would soon find myself caught up in sexual sin once again. However, this time seemed to be worse than ever before.

Reminded of the scripture, which says, "When the unclean spirit has gone out of a person, it passes through waterless places seeking rest, and finding none it says, 'I will return to my house from which I came.' In addition, when it comes, it finds the house swept and put in order. Then it goes and brings seven other spirits more evil than itself, and they enter and dwell there. And the last state of that person is worse than the first." (Luke 11:24-26)

I know this to be true because once I entered back into this sin it seems it took on a completely new form. If I told you how I tried with every ounce of my being to resist having sex with this man you would not believe it because with all of my effort, I should have been able to resist him.

The enemy was cunning, he knew exactly what I wanted and desired at that time. You must understand that guys were hitting on me constantly in that season but I was resisting them easily because they were not my desire and I did not want to mess up with God. Being blind-sided with a tall, dark, handsome, persistent brother would become my downfall.

He was exactly my desire and he refused to give up even though I kept denying him. I mean this man would not leave me alone. I kept telling him no, I could not be with him. Nevertheless, regardless of what I said or did, he remained faithful to the chase. After trying repeatedly to resist him, I could no longer resist. I finally wanted him more than he desired me. We ended up together and it was not long before I was in the fight of my life for chastity.

When I say I was in a fight, I mean that literally. I was warring in the spirit against sex demons. I was playing with major fire and it burned badly.

I reminisce on a time in the beginning when it all began. It started out by him coming over and we would spend quality time together. We were always together unless we were in class; he was in football practice or on the court shooting basketball. Everything was good until we started getting too close. We began lying in bed watching movies together and being alone in dark lit rooms. This was a huge mistake.

I remember the first time when this happened and things began to heat up. There were two people who had great passion and chemistry with one another, acting as if we were just common friends able to withstand the temptation. I must have been out of my mind to think I could resist him for too long when I was putting myself in a position to have the very thing I loved; sex.

We kissed and it escalated from there. Before I knew it, we were touching and grinding on top of each other. I was still fighting and resisting so our clothes remained on; but with each new encounter, it went a bit further. It became a game to see how close we could come to having sex without actually having it.

I became an expert at having sex without actually "having sex" so to speak. Trust me there is no such a thing as not having sex, other than not having sex. You may only be touching each other right now but soon, you will be fondling each other's genitals and putting them around sensitive areas to enjoy the sensation without going all the way. This is so dangerous to do. Trust me at some point you will be lost or caught up in the feeling and will end up having full-blown sex. You will try to stop yourself but it will feel too good to stop it.

This is what was happening in our relationship so we would often engage in sexual activity without having sex traditionally. We had come up with our own form of satisfying one another. The more I played with fire, the more it burned. You cannot play on the edge of a cliff without someday falling off if you get too close and that is what happened.

He played too close to the edge, far too long until he slipped into me; I allowed it occasionally for a few seconds then I would make him pull out. Before long, I was having sex with him for a few minutes before I would make him stop. It was not long before I found myself crying and broken constantly for being disobedient to God and falling prey to old habits consistently.

Being a sex junkie, is a lot like being a dope fiend. You cannot expect to be around it and taste just a little bit without eventually going all out. That is what happened to me. Just as there are consequences to drug use, there are consequences to having sex outside of marriage. Although I must say, anytime you have sex with a person whether or not you go before a judge or preacher you have married them in the spirit. The two of you have become one the moment you consummated your relationship in having sex.

When two people become one, they take on the characteristics of the other person. For instance, if you sleep with a liar, you may find yourself lying when you were never one to lie. It does not matter their downfall, you may fall prey to its affects. This is especially true for women considering we are receivers. Men are releasers; they release while we receive. The problem is men do not only release sperm but other things in the spiritual realm. They release any spirits they carry into us and we often times become like them.

This is why God intended for man and woman to have sex in the confines of marriage to only one person. When we indulge in multiple partners, we are never fully satisfied because we have tasted of too many varieties to settle on one flavor easily. Soul ties must be broken in order for these spiritual marriages to be broken. Otherwise, you remain connected to every person you have ever slept with and you wonder why you are confused. It is because you have too many people inside of you.

From experience, this can be devastating to you and your relationship; especially if you are being married for the first time in the natural but you are still married in the spirit to multiple partners. If you have not dissolved those spiritual relationships, you must pray today for release.

Back to the story at hand, all Satan needed was for me to fall one time to get what he wanted. His aim was to embarrass and discredit me as a Christian. He achieved it the moment the news broke of my pregnancy. I heard things like, "I knew she wasn't saved, she's just like us!" They were right; I was just like them in the sense that I was a sinner. However, I was a sinner saved by grace and I was in need of the grace of God more than ever at that point.

However, I was not like them in the sense that I was not just doing whatever I wanted to do. It was not easy for me to be in that predicament. I hated what I was doing but I had a serious problem and it was not easy to overcome it. I cried, hurt, and wanted to change and I would soon give up the relationship with my boyfriend as much as I loved him but I could not continue sinning against God.

I was tired of making the same mistake repeatedly and feeling guilty and ashamed to go before God in prayer. However, in a matter of weeks after ending the relationship, I found out I was pregnant. I was devastated. I wish I had stopped long before it escalated to sex and pregnancy but it was too late.

I went back to my child's father and we moved forward in our relationship. However, things would go sour rather quickly. I was soon hurt to find my Christian boyfriend drinking, partying, smoking weed and staying out late until the wee hours of the morning, against everything I had known of him.

I knew when we got together that he was not perfect. I knew that he used to be involved in all those things and that we were not on the same level. However, I was optimistic of him. He was living a clean life and I was proud of him. Yes, we had made mistakes together but I did not expect him to return to his old life.

I was shocked and hurt and I asked him to make a decision between those things and his baby and me. He literally broke my heart when he told me that was unable to stop doing the things he was doing. He said it was too much for him to deal with becoming a father and trying to maintain his relationship with God.

I broke up with him that day. I was so depressed and hurt and I pleaded with him not to abandon us. He said he was not abandoning me, I was abandoning him. How could I stay with him under the circumstances? He had changed so much since we found out that I was pregnant. He was no longer spending all of his time with me and he was treating me differently.

I was devastated, yet I refused to remain with him. I told him that he would regret his decision in the end. I told him he was losing a great woman. I reminded him that he still had responsibility to our child whether or not he wanted it. In my eyes, he had given up; leaving me to fight alone through my difficulties and depression and for that I hated him. No one knew my pain for I stood strong although I was extremely broken.

I began to contend with the murdering spirit that had latched on to me when I was sixteen and had my first abortion. I had to battle with the fact that I was pregnant and that the father had chosen other things over us, which caused me to leave him. I would ultimately have my child; a baby girl named Hope but not without facing one of the most difficult fights of my life.

I planned an abortion, set the appointment, and was ready to rid myself of my problem when God spoke to me not to harm my daughter. I was so afraid to hurt her after God spoke that to me, not to mention the resistance I had already met from my best friend that refused to go with me to have the abortion. She advised against the abortion and said if I were going to go through with it, she did not want to have anything to do with it. I was so angry with her but after having the baby, I was grateful for her resistance.

It was not until I was seven months pregnant that I finally accepted the fact that I was pregnant but I still was not happy about it. I did not feel the joy of pregnancy as most mothers had. I am still saddened about that to this day.

However, when my beautiful baby girl was born, I was much happier with the idea of being a mother. It was still difficult for me in the beginning but I soon found that my daughter's birth was one of the greatest joys of my life. What I felt during my pregnancy had nothing to do with her.

I was hurting, angry, fearful, and vindictive. I did not want to have a baby by her father because he had treated me so badly. He was never there for me throughout my pregnancy. In fact, he was on campus having sex with other women during that time. I was hurt by this and I wanted to hurt him as much as he was hurting me. I wanted him to cry as I did almost daily. I wanted him to know what it was like for someone to suddenly change and turn their backs on you.

He was the reason I could not connect with my child as she grew within me. I hated the half of him that grew within me as she reminded me of him. Throughout the pregnancy, I found peace in the arms of God. Had it not been for him, I would not have made it through it. God had mercy on me and kept me from harming the child or myself. My child's father remained selfish and unconcerned about the baby or me until after she was born.

He pursued me once again after Hope was born in an effort to become a family but I had too much anger and hurt in my heart to forgive him and take him back. He tried everything to get me to comply even gave me ultimatums but I stood my ground. I still loved him but I hated him too because of hurt, anger and bitterness. When I became pregnant, he became jealous and it escalated tremendously after my pregnancy. He kicked my door down and hit me all out of jealousy.

I recall the night he hit me. It was during a barbeque that was thrown by a mutual friend on campus; he grabbed me by my throat and threw me to concrete because I was talking to another man. I was stunned because he had never put his hands on me before. Not only that, I would soon find out he had been suspended from school on suspicion of rape.

Although it was later deemed a lie, I was hurt that he had lied to me about why he was suspended. These things in combination with how he treated me during my pregnancy caused me to refuse going back to him even though I loved him.

Back to my focus, the night our daughter was born, he was nowhere to be found. He was one of the last persons to know that she had been born. That was hurtful to me. When he finally showed up to the hospital, he was too late to sign the birth certificate. I harbored much resentment towards him and in some ways towards his daughter because she was a part of him.

However, after letting go of much of my hatred for him, I was able to love my daughter, as I should. She is such a blessing to my life. I would not change what I went through because she was a product of it. She has inspired me in so many ways. She taught me how to love unconditionally. She taught me the value of life, love, and happiness. She is a reflection of God.

Her father and I are friends today, thank God. I went on for many years holding resentment towards him especially after he was not there for our daughter as he should be. When he finally came around and began making efforts, it was difficult for me to allow it because I felt it was not fair. I had labored through the most difficult years of her life without him. Why should he be able to come in now and reap the benefits of my struggles? I felt he had no right.

However, God changed my heart towards him and I truly forgave him. He and his daughter have a great relationship now and we are friends as well. I thank God for healing my hurt and everything I held in my heart against him. I live free from any feelings of resentment towards him or anyone who has ever hurt me.

After my child's father and I went our separate ways, I would later go on to rededicate my life back to God and live on the straight and narrow but not before wasting more time chasing love; which was like chasing the wind, I could never obtain it.

Chapter 13
Men, Men, Men

After being hurt by my child's father and being unable or unwilling to forgive him, I found myself searching for the love I was desperately desiring. The enemy knew my desire for love and the extent I would go to get it and he set me up big time.

It seemed as though it was raining men. At every turn there was a man seeking me out. I could not go any place without meeting a man who was interested in me from the grocery store to the bank; you name it and I am sure I have met a man there.

I was sexy, young, and desirable. It was not hard to get a man; it was hard to get the right man. Either he was a liar, cheater, unsaved, or married. I could not catch a good break because all the men I was meeting were handsome, sexy, intelligent and desirable but something was always lacking in them. In fact, none of them wanted to be in an old-fashioned relationship where you would court and get married.

They wanted the modern day way of being together. Let us try out the goods, move in together and see if we like it and then we will get married if we like it. I was not feeling that. However, I began playing their silly game. My list of men were building up and I felt more like I was chasing a record of who can have the most men as opposed to chasing love.

I met guy after guy, dated one after another, and still had not found Mr. Right. I was getting deeper and deeper into bad situations until I found myself in the ultimate pickle. I ran into an old college mate that I was once interested in and had dated briefly, but we never had an intimate relationship.

One evening he came by my house to visit and we sat and talked. I never thought anything could happen between us because I knew he was married and I would never be with a married man, so I thought. Unfortunately, when I saw him, the flame we shared on our college campus was still burning bright and he was fanning it with all of his might.

Before the evening was up, we had become intimate and I felt awful. I wanted to die; I could not believe I would allow myself to be with a married man. In addition, because he felt awful for forcing himself on me, he decided to buy me a card, which I left at work; which was subsequently his job also, and it was big news as it passed around our office for all to see. I was very embarrassed.

It was obvious we had been intimate when he mentioned if I were pregnant that he would be there for the baby and me. I was the talk of the town on my job and I soon found married men pursuing me from every angle of the globe. There was a sign on me that read, "I sleep with married men" it seemed. I would soon find myself in that situation again unaware the man was married. I would break it off as soon as I found out.

Unfortunately, I met another married man who I would soon fall for after we spent a wonderful evening together talking over dinner. The attraction we shared was magnetic and I found him to be irresistible even while knowing he was married. I swear I was becoming sillier by the minute as I would fall in love with this man and spend the next year of my life with him knowing he was married.

During that time, I would get pregnant again; and unfortunately, the murdering spirit came upon me once again, but this time I would go through with the abortion, refusing to have a child with a married man. I soon broke the relationship off after that incident and moved on with my life.

I was callus and unaffected back then about having an abortion; but when healing finally came to my life, I would hurt tremendously because of what I had done. I would seek God's forgiveness and the forgiveness of my two aborted children, as well as from my surviving daughter who always wanted a brother or sister.

I am a mother of three but I only have one child to show for it because I murdered two of my children. I do not know their sexes; who they would have looked like, what gifts they would have had or how my life would have been different. All I can say is I miss them so much and I wish I could have them here with me. However, I am grateful that they are in a better place with my heavenly father who is taking excellent care of them. I am grateful that they do not have to experience the pain of this life, and all of the hurt that I have had to endure.

There is not a day that goes by that I do not think about my babies and regret my awful actions. I reiterate, I wish I could turn back the hands of time and make a different decision but I cannot. The only hope I have is in making it into heaven to see my babies again.

After this perverse relationship and horrible outcome, I knew it was time to get it together before I ended up dead and in hell. I ran back to God with a repentant heart and remained single until I met my husband.

If you have any question in your mind why I love God so much, what you have heard thus far should explain it. We serve an awesome God who is merciful, just, long-suffering and forgiving. If it had been anyone else, they would have given up on me a long time ago, but God never gave up on me. Through all of my disobedience and mistakes, He remained faithful and loving towards me. I could never forget His love or forgiveness towards me. The Bible says, "Therefore, I tell you, her many sins have been forgiven--for she loved much. But he, who has been forgiven little, loves little." (Luke 7:47) God has forgiven me much so I love Him much.

Chapter 14
Failed Marriage

I met my husband because of my daughter's love for gum. We were at a conference at my church where I was preparing to lead worship that night. My husband had come out as a guest of my musician. He arrived early that night before the service began while I was in the sanctuary preparing.

My daughter who never meets a stranger, and used to scare me half to death by just walking up to random people and being her naturally friendly self, went up to him and asked if he had any gum. He proceeded to ask, "Whose adorable daughter is this?"

I responded. "Oh that would be mine. I'm sorry, what is she doing, asking you for gum?"

"Yes she is."

"I knew it because she loves gum and is always seeking it."

"Oh that's ok, she isn't bothering me, and she is really polite and sweet."

"Thank you."

"What is her name?"

I turned to Hope, "Tell him your name."

"Hope"

"Aw, she is so adorable, simply gorgeous."

"Thank you, well I am going to take her up to the stage with me and get her out of your hair."

"Oh she's fine; it's not a problem at all."

I smiled and walked away. Little did I know, we would be married a little over a year later from that chance encounter. We did not exchange numbers that night or even express any interest in each other at that time. It was not until a week later that I would see him again at a musician's rehearsal.

We met again that night and when the rehearsal was finished; we sat and talked for hours finding out that we had much in common; especially spiritually. We had the same vision, goals and dreams involving ministry. We loved God equally and our entire conversation had centered on that.

Ladies please be aware that just because a man is a Christian, and seems to fit your ideal man, it does not mean that he is the man that God has destined for your life. I had to learn that the hard way. Take it from me, it is no fun; so please do not do it. Wait on the Lord and do not ignore any warning signs.

We would go on to speaking on the phone and during those times, we would worship and pray together. It was beautiful. It was my first time ever sharing my faith like that with a boyfriend and I loved it. Satan knew he could not get me any other way except through a Godly man. Yes, Satan can use Godly people if they allow him too. He knew that I was not settling for anything less and he set me up.

Do not get me wrong, God warned me in two dreams, through a stranger and through some incidences involving jealousy before we got married but I did not take heed. I was tired of being alone and I wanted to be married so I could legally have sex and be pleasing to God. Besides he wined and dined me and showed me a type of love I had not ever experienced before. He did the sweetest things for me and treated me like a queen the entire time we were courting. I fell in love, so when he proposed to me, I quickly said yes. I was the happiest woman alive.

Prior to us getting married however, tragedy struck. My daughter Hope was diagnosed with Type I diabetes nine days before her fourth birthday. I was devastated. How could this be when God told me to have her?

This was unfair when God told me not to harm her. How could he allow Satan to harm her? I was angry with God. I wanted answers and her healing to come forth. I saw her suffer some serious and scary attacks. In the beginning, she had an episode one night shortly after going to bed. She woke up crying and I immediately went into the bedroom to see about her.

When I arrived, she was sitting up in bed whining. I asked her if she was ok but she did not respond. I asked her if she needed to use the bathroom. She said yes and I took her into the bathroom. There as she sat on the toilet she began having convulsions. I was afraid and unsure what to do. It was her first episode and I was terrified. Thank God, my fiancé was there to help.

I cleaned her up and removed her from the toilet, and took her into the living room where my fiancé was. I was shaking, crying, and unable to gather my composure. She was crying and screaming, "No, no, leave me alone." I said baby what do I do? My fiancé said give her to me baby; and calm down; it is going to be ok.

Hope continued to scream and reached for me saying mommy. I took her into my arms, cried, and prayed. She then reached for my fiancé while crying and saying, "Daddy" My fiancé calmly took her into his arms and began to stroke her gently and telling me to calm down. He said, "Go and get what you need for her."

I went to get the glucose gel and fed it to her. After a while, she began to come back to herself. I was relieved as she began to smile and play with us as if nothing had happened at all. God knew I could not have handled that on my own that night. I am grateful to God for allowing my fiancé to be there.

God has been merciful and Hope has not been hospitalized since her initial diagnosis. However, she did have a major episode one night while I was visiting a friend's home for a business meeting. The wife of my producer's business partner cooked some fajitas and offered us some. I did not want any but Hope had some. That night, unbeknownst to me, Hope provided too much insulin to herself, which caused her blood sugar to plunge.

When I was about to leave, I noticed that Hope sat on the couch unresponsive, which was an immediate red flag. I asked for a soda and began trying to give it to her. Unfortunately, she was already too far gone to drink. My last effort to give her something to drink sent her into convulsions and then a full-blown seizure.

It was awful, I had never seen her have a seizure before and I almost passed out watching it. I cried and screamed someone please call 911. The seizure lasted about minute but felt like hours. Her eyes rolled in the back of her head, she shook uncontrollably as her small frame appeared to be tossed around by an unseen force. When the attack was over, she was stuck in a deformed position and she struggled to breathe, as she wheezed in a low tone. It was scary. I began to pray and hold her in my arms until the ambulance arrived. When the ambulance and fire-truck arrived, she was still a bit unresponsive.

The medic placed an oxygen mask on her face to help her breathe and she kept removing it. Next, they tried to feed her a peanut butter sandwich but she refused to eat from them. They asked her if I could feed it to her and she agreed. As I fed her the sandwich, the child stop mid-bite and said, "Hey where's the jelly?" We all laughed and said, "She's back!" It was great seeing my baby responsive and being the character that she normally is.

I have believed God for her healing for over nine years now but I have not given up hope. I am still standing on His promises concerning her healing. Through it all, God has been faithful. He has been good to the both of us and I do not take His provision and mercy lightly.

Now back to the proposal and marriage. The fairy tale wedding I dreamed about would soon turn into a simple ceremony and a honeymoon I would better describe as a "Sour-moon." Our blissful life together started out extremely wrong and I was completely unhappy. I should have had the marriage annulled but I was hoping it was just a rocky start.

I was wrong, things grew increasingly worse.

During our honeymoon, we had an incident to occur which provoked a separation between us. I would soon go home but things would never be the same. My husband became controlling, mean, and demanding. There were many double standards involved in our relationship and I was ultimately broken down to the lowest level a woman could be broken. I was being abused, and did not know it.

My family was concerned about me and how I had changed and I heard things like, "You are different; you don't smile, joke or dress like you used to. You seem like a different person; we do not know who you are anymore." I was lost and unable to see my way. I lost all of my confidence, my self-esteem was extremely low, and I did not know who I was any more.

I was soon isolated from family and friends and treated like a prisoner in my own home. I was so unhappy I used to cry myself to sleep or crawl up in a ball underneath the bathroom cabinet and weep. I would sit in the closet for hours and cry, moan and pray for healing and peace. I was in bad shape.

My husband was mean and uncaring. He didn't care about my feelings or what I thought about anything in our home. His only concern was his happiness. My husband would be nice one minute and the next, be so mean I wasn't sure who he was. He would get angry and leave the house for days at a time without answering any of my phone calls.

He would demean me in one breath and request sex in the next. He would withhold money, sex, and conversation from me to "punish me" when he was upset. I hardly ever asked for any money but when I did, he would say we didn't have any but there were thousands of dollars sitting in our account. When I would mention the money, he would say we are saving. However, that same day or the next, if he wanted something, he would purchase it no matter how much it would cost him.

What hurt me tremendously was his response when it was time to purchase supplies for my daughter. Because my husband made too much money, we had to pay for everything out of pocket for my daughter's diabetes. We had to pay for the doctor's visits which were anywhere from $300 to $800 a visit (depending on what was being done) and she had to go every three months. Her test strips were $90 a bottle, and we needed those twice a month. In addition to that, she needed insulin which costs $120 a vial, and we needed at least two of those a month. Not to mention the syringes we had to purchase for her to take the shots.

I know it was expensive and very taxing for him to support our home and her condition financially, but it did not make me feel any better when I would be fussed at when I had to let him know that we needed something. I will admit he was a wonderful father and provider.

The problem was he was so stuck on providing financially that he neglected me emotionally. However, he treated my daughter with great respect and love. If he could have treated me the way he treated her, we would probably still be together today. I know that Hope was one of the reasons I stayed in our marriage so long. I wanted her to have what I never had, a father in the home.

I thank God for him being there for her growing up and still to this day. He still provides for her and continues to be a part of her life.

After all, he helped me raise her and she loves him.

So back to what I was saying, he was not there for me financially when it came to something personal I wanted although I hardly ever asked for anything. The crazy thing about that was he did not want me to work, but I was tired of feeling as if I didn't have any means or support.

I decided to go back to work. I finally convinced him to allow me to, but it came with some conditions. I was told that I would still be responsible for the house entirely as if I were not working, including cooking meals daily. Anything I had done prior to working, I was required to continue to do with a job.

He was never supportive of me or my endeavors. He often discouraged me from moving forward in pursuing any of my dreams, especially singing. He did not want to see me get ahead because he felt he would lose his control over me. He would rejoice for me as long as the accomplishment was minute but if it were on a larger scale, he would not support it or rejoice concerning it.

I was constantly accused of cheating. I couldn't even be a few minutes late coming home from work or the grocery store without being accused of seeing someone else. Even if I were only five minutes late, I had to have stopped off and gotten a "Quickie."

I was confused about how to behave at church because one minute I was being too nice and the next I was being anti-social according to him. I could never please him. It got so bad; I was not allowed to go to church with him anymore because we were constantly fighting about some guy in the church looking at me or disrespecting him etc.

The crazy thing was, in front of people, he treated me like a queen but behind closed doors, I was treated like manure. I promise, I felt like I was losing my mind. Even when he would do nice things for me, it would still seem so cold and careless. It was as if he felt I should be happy for what I was getting. I hated his smug attitude. He thought he was better than I was. He made good money, had a little prestige, and knew the word of God so he acted as if he had it all over me.

He made me feel like I was not good enough to have what he had and trust me, everything we had was his according to him. He often said things like, "This is my house, or my car." I was so tired of his king of the castle routine. I was tired of him treating me like a second-class citizen.

I was criticized for the food being cold when it was his fault for being late. I was called on my job if something was left undone in the house even something as small as a fork or spoon being left in the sink or the bed being left unmade when I was in a hurry.

I recall having a Honda Accord that had a very bad oil and water leak and it would cause the car to run hot if I didn't replenish it. My husband had a new truck with no problems whatsoever, but he would not allow me to drive it to work. Instead, he allowed me to become stranded on the side of the road several times at night, and would get angry when I would call him for help. I endured so many awful things during my marriage and I could go on and on, but I feel this overview gives enough insight into the marriage that you can easily tell I was miserable.

Besides, he is a man of God (Back then he was one with many issues, that he needed to be delivered from) and I would not dare try to judge him or ruin his reputation. He has acknowledged his wrong and repented for his wrongdoing and I have forgiven him.

We endured a long separation after a couple of short term ones. Four years after being married to the man I thought was the man for me, we would be divorced. Unlike most women who go through a divorce, I was happy. I was sad because I did not approve of divorce but equally happy because I did not approve of being married to a man who treated me as if I were less than human.

I will not pretend to have been perfect in our marriage, but I can say that I tried with everything in me to honor him. I loved him and wanted my marriage to survive. Unfortunately, it did not. I too made mistakes, but they were usually a reaction to an action. I was provoked to uncharacteristic behaviors because of anger, hurt and disappointment.

I became jealous and suspicious because of his actions towards me and I was sure he was cheating; although I did not have any proof. I would become so angry with him until I wanted to kill him, but God helped me to overcome my hatred towards him and withheld my hand against him.

I did not understand why he was treating me so badly, but I had to take into account that a person has to reap what they have sown. Now if you recall the awful mistakes I made when I was in a relationship with a married man for an entire year; I was reaping what I had sown. I believe my marriage failed partly because of what I had done in my past. The other part, was due to unforgiveness, and issues we both had that kept us from being what we needed to be for one another.

A few months following our divorce, I would go through counseling for eight months and it changed my life completely. I was healed from things that happened to me when I was a little girl and throughout my life. I was freed from negative mindsets about myself, God, and others. I learned to value myself, and esteem God in my life, above all else.

I learned the power of forgiveness, and the importance of forgiving oneself. I learned that the only person that I need to affirm me is God. I learned how to live without the pain of insecurity and the negative effects of low self-esteem. I was taught to be slow to anger, by using the life tools I was given throughout the sessions.

I pray that you will seek help if you are struggling with issues. Many people view counseling as a negative thing, when in fact it is a wonderful tool of change. However, in the African American community, it is frowned upon in some circles. Do not be deterred from receiving help. If you want change, and an opportunity to change is given, embrace it. It may be the difference between a joyous life, and one of misery.

I recommend counseling to all those who need it. However, pray and ask God to lead you to the right counselor, because in the hands of the wrong person, things can become worse. I know because I experienced that with my first counselor. I quickly ended all sessions with her because she was making me feel worse.

My heart goes out to those of you who are broken, depressed, living in shame, and struggling with unforgiveness, because of the pain of your past. My heart also goes out to those of you who are entangled in immoral situations that are setting you up, for future disappointment. I pray that you will make a conscious decision to change. I pray that you

will allow the power of the Lord Jesus
Christ, to set you free. He came to
set the captives free. He is willing,
and able to release you from your
bondage if you would only ask Him.

I pray that if you are in a
relationship with someone else's
spouse that you would repent, and
walk away from that adulterous
relationship, before it is too late. I
pray that God will have mercy on you
if you are not married, and have a
desire to be married, in the future. I
pray that you will turn to God, and
follow his will, and his way for your
life. I pray that you will prosper, and
be in health. I pray that you will
forgive others, and be forgiven.

I was so blessed after making
up my mind to forgive my ex-
husband. Five years after our divorce,
my husband apologized to me for
hurting me, and gave me the much-
needed closure, that brought great
peace to my heart. It also confirmed
what I had believed all along,
concerning what caused our demise. I
thank God for touching his heart to
do it.

God knew my heart. I forgave,
and released him from the all
judgments I previously held against
him. I forgave him for the hurt that

he caused me, and asked God to bless him. The moment I did that, God touched his heart to give me closure. Is not God good? He is so awesome in all of His ways!

All that I have shared with you in the pages of this book is only a representation of my life. It would take a series of books to explain in detail the pain I experienced over the course of my life. However, it is not necessary to re-live the pain of my past in detail. I have shared enough of what I experienced to get the point across of God's goodness, mercy, forgiveness, longsuffering and love.

I am grateful for this opportunity to share my life, and my testimony with others in an effort to encourage, uplift, and bless them, by what God has done for me and will do for them. I pray that your lives will never be the same after reading this book and welcoming God into your situation to help you overcome in every area of your lives.

Epilogue

I have to end this book on a positive note. I dare not speak of my pain and not mention the joys of my life! I must tell of the goodness of Jesus and all that He has done for me, because without Him I would not have accomplished anything. He is the reason for my success.

You are looking at a woman who had great insecurities and very low self-esteem, but in the midst of it all, I accomplished much. How was I able to accomplish such greatness? God alone helped me. Whenever I endeavored to do something, I prayed and asked God for His help, and I still do that even now. I asked for His help in writing this book.

God is faithful in being there when we invite Him into our lives and situations. So let me share some of the things I have accomplished with God's help. I guess I will start with high school accomplishments. My first year, I was voted Ms. Charlie Company in JROTC, despite my fears and insecurities. This was a major accomplishment; an honor a freshman usually does not achieve.

Secondly, I tried out for cheerleading and although I was terrified, I made the squad. Each year we had to try out to continue on the squad and each year I made it. I would go on to become the captain of the cheerleaders my senior year. That was also a major accomplishment because of the other great competitors in the running.

Thirdly, while in theatre arts my freshman year, I won a leading role for the productions that year "A Raison in the Sun." I later had to drop out of theatre arts for cheerleading the following year, but I never lost my passion for it.

In addition, as a freshman, I auditioned to be in the concert choir (which was reserved for sophomores through seniors) but I was awarded a spot in the choir that year. This was a huge deal because I was terrified of singing in front of others. I will never forget walking into that choir room and almost passing out, when Mr. William Mitchell asked me to sing my audition song in front of the entire 50-member choir. With another young woman's help, I was able to sing a portion of a song and it went well.

In addition to that, Mr. Mitchell caused me to break out of my shy shell and sing my first solo in front of a huge audience at our spring musical during that year. It was because of this that I went on to sing with other community choirs and groups, landing solo parts in them all.

I would also later become the Vice President of the concert choir my junior year and President my senior year. I achieved many other awards such as perfect attendance throughout high school, as well as academic achievement awards. I was also voted most talented my senior year by my peers, and was blessed to lead the class song at our graduation.

I graduated with honors and was in the top percentile of my class. In addition to that, I was awarded two scholarships, one to Navarro Junior College and the other to Clark-Atlanta University for music. However, I would not use either scholarship. Instead, I went to Texas A&M University (Formally known as East Texas State University). There I graduated with a B.S. Degree in Criminal Justice. I achieved the Dean's List twice and graduated with honors (A member of the National Criminal Justice Honor Society; Secretary of my chapter).

This was a huge feat after starting out rocky and being on academic probation, but God saw me through it. I cried many of nights and asked for His help and He helped me. Not only to pass, but also to pass with excellence and graduate with honors, God is good!

I have realized many awesome dreams. I have formed my own singing groups; written original music; recorded my own project in the studio and recorded with other artists as well. I have written, directed and produced stage plays, as well as written poetry and books. I have now become an entrepreneur, something I never thought possible.

I am a living witness that when you put God first, He will bless you. I was so afraid to start my own business for many years until God blessed me with the confidence to step out and trust Him. One can never achieve unless they believe in themselves. I did not know how to believe in myself; I had no self-esteem but I have found my esteem in God and it enables me to do things I never thought possible. I do everything in the strength of God.

I truly believe that I can do all things through Christ who gives me the strength to do it. I live by this motto and all the other wisdom the word of God has to offer. I could go on about other achievements but I believe this gives God adequate praise for all He has done for me. I am forever grateful for His love, protection, favor, and peace throughout my life.

I pray for each of you who have not experienced the help of God in your everyday life to come to the knowledge of God's help in life's situations. It is a blessing having someone to turn to that you can depend on in your times of need.

If you have not tried Jesus, I suggest you do because He is a faithful friend. He is not a spiritual Santa Clause, but a faithful friend. Develop a relationship with him and you will reap the benefits of that relationship in every area of your lives. I honestly do not know how anyone can live without Him.

I am so excited about this book and the possibilities of what it may accomplish in the lives of those who read it until I am overjoyed.

This is one of many books to come that I will write to educate, enlighten, enhance, inspire and uplift others. I have truly enjoyed writing my testimony in the pages of this book. I was so afraid to put this information on paper as an open book; but God has given me peace about it. I am ready to share my life with others in an effort to give life to others.

The purpose of this book is to show the mercy, grace and forgiveness of God. He had great mercy on me in the midst of all of my mistakes. He was longsuffering with me. Most of all He never gave up on me, even when I was sinking deep in my sin. I am forever grateful for His love.

This is my testimony of deliverance. I am not perfect by a long shot, but He who has saved me is perfect and He uses imperfect people like me, to minister a perfect gospel. Jesus Christ is a savior, healer, deliverer, redeemer, and restorer. Whatever you need him to be in your situation, He is! He is the Great I Am! Call on Him today for salvation, for healing, for deliverance. Do not be afraid or ashamed. He loves you and wants to be there for you. Nothing you have done is too bad; there is no problem too hard for Him to fix. If you call on Him He will answer; and save and heal you. Try Him today!

Please know that even when you submit your life to Christ, you will still face difficulties, but I promise it becomes a lot easier to face problems and issues with Him than without Him. I pray that you come to know Him intimately and receive all of His love for you.

I pray that every individual who has read this book felt the presence of God and has a better understanding of our enemy. I pray that you will take from this reading experience, that there is hope for you in your situation regardless of what it is. If God has delivered me, surely He will do the same for you. He loves you, just as much as He loves me.

Thank you for taking this journey of life with me, through reading this book. I pray that you walk away with a better sense of who you are as it relates to Jesus Christ, and who you can become through His healing power. May God Bless You All, in the Name of Jesus!

About the Author

Shameka Bonner is a multi-talented individual who enjoys writing books, poetry, scripts, and songs. She also loves to sing, and produce music and seeks to develop her writing skills to include screenplays in the future. She is the Founder and Artistic Director of United Christian Artists Talent Agency.

Prior to becoming an entrepreneur, Shameka worked in various fields such as Criminal Justice, Teaching, and Insurance. Shameka holds a Bachelor of Science Degree in Criminal Justice from Texas A&M University in Commerce, Texas. She is a devout Christian and spends most of her time dedicated to the work of the ministry, by ministering the gospel through the arts in a real and interesting way.

She prays this book enlightens, encourages, and brings healing to those who have been abandoned, abused, betrayed, broken, confused, and misused. She prays that the backslidden will return to Christ and the sex-addict be delivered in Jesus name, Amen.

Final Words

"May the peace of God and His delivering power rescue you from the clutches of whatever stronghold is holding you captive. It is my prayer that you become all that God has destined for you to become in this life, fulfilling His purpose and destiny in your life in Jesus' name I pray; amen!"

Lovingly,

-Shameka

42523561R00094

Made in the USA
San Bernardino, CA
04 December 2016